Phases

of our

Lives

A FAMILY CHRONICLE

WOLFGANG AND FRANCESCA MACK

WAMFAM PRESS
2016

Phases of our Lives

"Phases of our Lives - A Family Chronicle"
1st Edition
By Wolfgang and Francesca Mack
Edisted by Francesca Mack

Published by WAMFAM Press
1301 Spring Street, Suite 28H
Seattle WA, 98104

Images in the text by Wolfgang Mack
and by permission from Landesarchiv Baden-
Wuerttemberg

Library of Congress Control Number: 2016905110
ISBN-13: 978-1530391790
ISBN-10: 1530391792
BISAC:Biography and Autobiography/Personal Memoirs

Printed in the USA

Also by the Author:

"In Search of a New Morality"
"Memories and Lessons from my Young Years in Wartime
Germany"

PHASES OF OUR LIVES

Acknowledgment

This book is dedicated to our wonderful grandchildren, Audrey and Adam, Adeline, Anderson and Adrian, Lily and Lucas, and Sophia, Little Wolf, Roland and Conrad, in the hope that one day they will find it interesting to read about the times when their grandparents grew up, and what it took for them to lay the foundation for the family that is their heritage. Hopefully, this book will help them and all my readers to better understand their own origins and how they fit in to the larger context of history.

In putting together my stories I had the good fortune of invaluable encouragement from friends and from my family and the benefit of their own thoughts. I owe all of them many thanks for their constructive contributions and their patience with my endeavors.

I owe a very special thanks to my lovely wife Francesca for her tireless editing and for her many suggestions and improvements. And without our son Christoph's help leading me into the electronic age, I could not have managed to get this book done.

Seattle, in the Autumn of our lives, 2016

Prologue

*"Love is God's most favorite gift, and then He
sends us into His big wide world to find it."*
Joseph von Eichendorff, 1788-1857

Some time ago our little granddaughter had come to me and said, "Omi told me you had been in a war. What was it like? Were you scared?"

"Yes, my little one. There was a terrible war way back when I was still a boy growing up in Germany. And yes, I was very scared, many times. And also, there was very little to eat, and often people were very mean to each other."

"But how did you come to America?"

"Well, I studied hard and they gave me a scholarship to study here, too".

"And how did you meet Omi?"

"Oh, that is quite a story: I met her in the sky. Really! She was an air hostess and I was a passenger!"

And so it went, until I decided to write it all down, for our sons and our wonderful grandchildren to know about the many adventures in Omi's and my life.

Some of the stories of my life in war time Germany may be difficult to fully understand for those who have never had to cope with political terror, with the horrors of the war, with hunger and deprivation. But people living in the comfort and freedom of our days should take out some time to try to understand.

In many ways I came out of all that with the best of all worlds - becoming more self-sufficient in many ways, getting to know

America, finding the right jobs for me to make a good living, and above all, finding the right spouse to share my life and to build a family of our own.

Nothing was a simple straight path. We had to find our way through a very competitive business world, through bringing up four healthy and vivacious sons, and to see them form their own families.

Surely you are not surprised that I wanted to write about the many phases of our life so that you can better remember, and perhaps learn something from the trials and tribulations of my young life, and the wonderful life your Omi and I lived together - and with you.

<O>

Phases of our Lives

A Boy Growing up

Phases of our Lives

Gengenbach - my Home Town

Ancient, prosperous and exceptional in many ways, a jewel set in the lovely foothills of the majestic Black Forest mountain range, medieval in its origins, but very much a part of modern life. Across

the valley is the great city of Strasbourg in nearby France, just a dozen miles away across the majestic Rhine river, which played such a pivotal role in the history of Europe. Sometimes, on a clear day, you can see the towering snow-capped peaks of the Swiss Alps. The hill-side vineyards frame the lovely Kinzig river valley, with its abundant fruit trees, berry farms and neatly tended fields. It was a great place for families to raise their children, and a good, if modest, place to live a healthy life.

There, life started out well enough for me. The traditional ringing of the ancient Gengenbach fortress bell announced the arrival of the Mayor's third son, ten and eleven years after brothers Hermann and Waldemar, and a year after him sister Anneliese, short for 'Anna Elisabeth Katharina Margot.' There were 13 pounds of me, feet first, with considerable doubt whether I would make it into this world, and so I got baptized twice - once barely emerged, on my feet, by our family friend, Dr. Waechter, and then again, a few weeks

later, in our magnificent Baroque church with all the pomp due a prominent Gengenbach family like ours.

I would be known adoringly as 'Woelfle' which is my name in our Alemanic dialect's diminutive, and not so flatteringly as 'Brummler' when I would mouth my dislikes, and occasionally also as 'Fresser' (not so complimentary either), when I would gulp down my food unceremoniously on the rare occasions when there was plenty of it.

But for the rest, everything of importance lined up well for me - a well respected family of some modest but comfortable means, quite sophisticated by standards of our small historic town, and, as time would tell, with good, durable genes, to boot. Life was good for our family. Thus the first few years provided me a solid base of

physical health, emotional stability, and mental development.

As the town's mayor Father was not only the representative of the authority, their civic leader, but his family also expected to set the social tone of the town. We lived accordingly, in the vast top floor of the Rathaus, that had been built in 1786 with civic pride, in the neoclassical style of a renaissance palace, quite a bit beyond the otherwise modest architecture of the town.

He was much admired for his leadership and his tireless efforts to ease the pains of the lost war, the devastating hyper-inflation that had wiped out most of the German middle class. Like many other mayors he even established Gengenbach's own local currency that succeeded to alleviate the terrible poverty of the dispossessed by getting the local economy going again. It opened up opportunities to tackle public works, like building new roads through the old hillside vineyards to make life easier for the wintners, modernize the public schools and the hospital that was in a stately building from the 1600s but in bad need of repair. These

projects also helped to re-awaken a sense of civic pride during a time when so many Germans were in a deep depression, not only economically, reeling from a horrible war and the verdict by the international community that Germany alone was to blame for the war and its devastations. Above all, Father put hundreds of the town's poor back into meaningful jobs. Without question, father was their leader and showed his real patriotism by relentlessly pursuing the public good.

In the twelve years under his leadership the people of Gengenbach started to prosper again, and just about everyone wanted him to continue as their leader indefinitely.

Life was good for the Mack family.

<O>

Nazi Terror

"The best political weapon is the weapon of terror"

- Heinrich Himmler, Chief of the Nazi Secret Police (GESTAPO)

Then, abruptly, in 1933, when I was just four, the world outside our family fell apart, with one disaster after another for the next fifteen years. The Hitler party had taken over the German government, and with them came the Nazi's suppression of anything and anybody who would stand in their way. The Nazi party terrorized all Germans with its private militia, the infamous 'Sturmabteilung' (the SA), intimidating and brutally beating anyone who dared to oppose them. This SA was a collection of rowdies and the disgruntled that seemed to hate everybody that stood for law and order. The Jewish population was their preferred scapegoat for all  the ills of the times, the lost war, the awful German economic depression and runaway inflation. The Nazis seemed eager for the next great war to start, which would eventually destroy Germany and condemn all of Europe to a daily fight for food, shelter in a seemingly endless struggle for survival.

Father had been relentless in his fight for a peaceful democratic Germany. He was a patriot of the best kind, having served honorably in the 'Great War' of 1914 and had seen enough of its horrors to do everything in his power to make sure that this would never happen again. All this was against everything the Nazis wanted. No wonder Father wound up as one of their targets to be eliminated, but his faith in justice and honor of the German people was such that he could not conceive that the Nazis would really go after him and do him harm.

But things got much worse all over Germany. Finally, Father agreed to get together with his fellow local leaders who all had been warned about the danger of getting arrested, but for what, did they ask each other? We have done nothing wrong, certainly nothing illegal! By that time, they all finally understood that their safety, and that of their families, were indeed at great risk. After some stormy arguments like: "we are not running away from them, this is preposterous, illegal, and un-German!" they saw no way out. They hastily packed a few necessities, and under cover of the night went to a timber-cutters' shed deep in the Black Forest, owned by of one of the other town's mayors, abandoned for the winter season.

Here, they hoped to wait a few days, to see whether the Nazi mob would simmer down, and if not, they would make their way to Switzerland by hiking on back roads. To their shock and surprise, they found themselves surrounded the next morning by the very mob they had tried to evade. They were hauled back to town and thrown into the Offenburg jail. Now the Nazis had their 'proof' - they accused these hapless, would-be escapees of treason! It was a huge blow for Father to be incarcerated - he, who always had upheld the principles of justice and freedom! He, who had fought valiantly to defend anyone threatened by Germany's growing mob mentality. At least he was not being ill treated - the prison staff knew him, and they had not yet been been perverted into what was to come in later years. But even the Nazis could not make their trumped-up charges stick in the courts. The German justice system was still working, though not for much longer. Luckily Father was released from jail after a few agonizing weeks.

Somebody obviously had told the 'authorities' of the mayors' escape plan, and to this date the identity of the informer remains a mystery. Of the three Nazi friends that knew the plan, only one survived the war: he maintained to his death that he had not betrayed them; yes, he was at that time a Nazi, but later changed his views when he saw the horrors of their regime. Besides, he was a loyal friend, and our families were very close. Many years later his son, without any prompting from our side, emphatically defended his father's innocence, telling us that his father, to the end, lived under the burden that his good friend, Eduard Mack, probably suspected him, no matter how much he assured him of his innocence. The plain fact is that there was a betrayal. This is just one of the innumerable personal tragedies that are born by political terror, in Germany, and anywhere in this world, wherever it is allowed to take root.

Where were all these proud Burghers when the Nazi mob descended on their towns and arrested their leaders? They did what so many in Germany, and in other places on this earth do when faced by lawlessness and the threat of physical harm. They retreated into what they thought was the safety of their homes and stayed quiet, heads in the sand, trying not to attract the ire of the mob. And there were many seemingly 'good' Germans, who changed their allegiance over to the Hitler party, some because they hoped for salvation from the ills of the dismal post-war times, and some because it was the convenient thing to do. To protect their careers, their comfort, they threw in with the tide of Nazism, ignoring dire warnings from people like Father. Many found out, to their great dismay, that this would not save them anyway.

It hurt Father immensely to be abandoned by the very people he had served so loyally in the difficult times after the Great War. He had helped them through the devastating German hyperinflation, the deep depression of the later 1920's, and the rising political violence of the early thirties, only to watch too many of his townspeople join in support of the evil Nazi regime. This story repeated itself a thousand times over throughout Germany, in the Nazis' exhilaration to enforce their newfound unchallenged power.

Life for us youngsters became clearly divided into two very separate spheres: an orderly, pleasant life inside the family, and a turbulent one every where else. There were the rules and the moral convictions of the family, expressed in no uncertain terms by my father and the quiet determination of my mother to maintain an orderly and caring home. There were lively, often passionate discussions about the outside world, the increasing Nazi oppression of "people like us," but we were also very much aware that nothing so freely discussed inside the family could ever be repeated, or even alluded to, to any one outside.

At first, being still little children we did not understand what was going on around us. As little ones, sister Anneliese and I were inseparable. At one Saturday afternoon, after school, Anneliese and her best friend, Sonia Matt, got the idea to go swimming in the town indoor pool in the center of Karlsruhe. At that time, even little children (I was seven) could freely get around the city unescorted. But on Saturdays the baths were reserved for women only. I was distraught not to be able to go with them. Anneliese had an idea: "You just wear one of our bathing suits and we will just say you are our younger sister". No problem, I thought in my innocence. But one look by the woman attendant was enough to 'blow my cover', and she threw us all out. I was incensed, and in my humiliation I shouted at her "you can shove your stupid bath...."At least I thought it would help me get rid of my fury, but the effect was that we did not dare set foot into the pool again. It showed me at a very early age that giving in to the urge to vent anger may satisfy my need to tell people off, but it would also shut the door to getting what you want at a later date. Control yourself!

Once we were a little older we could see the relentless indoctrination efforts by the Nazi propaganda machine, force-feeding the German people an endless succession of lies. We could see, increasingly, the physical signs of the growing Nazi terror, the arrests, the beatings, the quiet disappearing of people we knew, people who dared to voice their opposition to the Nazis. Like so many other Germans, our family had to make the hard decisions either to continue to speak our rejection of Nazism, or to behave more cautiously, and maybe survive. Even mildly criticizing the Nazis was not allowed, and penalties were severe. It was a constant 'tight rope' dance.

For the average German, it was getting very complicated. Should all German have revolted at enormous risk for their and their families' existence? Easy to judge from the perspective of a free nation that had never experienced political terror of this magnitude.

That, in a nutshell, would describe the way I saw my world as a young boy.

Phases of our Lives

Life under the the Nazi Regime

Like all dictators, the Nazis just about perfected the many ways to blunt any remaining resistance to their regime. The threat of being hauled in for 'interrogation' was bad already. Everybody knew what that would mean. The fear of winding up in concentration camp was enough to bend the will of the strongest. We knew that the camps existed, and we knew that they were awful, but few knew the full extent of their horrors until after the war. Another devilishly effective way the Nazis beat people into submission was to simply withhold rationing cards. Without a ration card, it was completely impossible to live.

Then the Nazis introduced the particularly odious practice of "Sippenhaft," making your relatives legally responsible for your compliance. What a frightening thought that your father or mother or brother or sister could be hauled away for your alleged misdeeds! In these ways, even the strongest would bend to their will. These threats to family members were in fact even more effective than the actual terror acts. Denouncements, with truly dire consequences, happened all the time, and were perhaps the most effective method of controlling the populace. Children denounced parents, businessmen denounced competitors, employees denounced rivals -

treachery was everywhere. It was easy; any little whisper was enough to get you hauled in for 'interrogation', and even if you were set free, you were branded as an enemy of the Vaterland. To get a feel for this mentality, watch "The Lives of Others," a movie set in post-war Communist East Germany. It could just as well have shown our life under the Nazi terror. No wonder we became fearful and suspicious - you couldn't trust anybody. But I, for one, was determined not to let fear circumscribe my life.

By the way, do you know how Germans would greet each other during the Nazi regime? If you guess the infamous "Heil Hitler," you are only partly right. Before saying "hello," or engaging somebody in a conversation, you would furtively look back over your shoulder to see whether anybody was close enough to eavesdrop on your conversation. This habit became second nature to many, and earned it the sardonic moniker, "der deutsche Gruss" (the German way of greeting). No joke. You simply could not trust anybody, period. Children were encouraged to inform on their parents, friends were set upon friends. The effect was utterly demoralizing.

While Father was still in the Offenburg prison we were evicted from our grand Rathaus residence. Mama and her four children would have literally been out in the street, but Father's relatives intervened: they helped us move into a reasonably comfortable apartment in Karlsruhe, then the State capital, where we were ordered to stay, along with many others that were designated as "unreliable persons requiring police surveillance." Here, after Father's release a few weeks later, the family settled in for an uneasy life marked by fear of making any misstep that would give new reason for being taken in for questioning. And for the first time, our family was dreadfully poor. Above all, Father had a hard time getting over his dismissal and the injustice he and his family had been forced to endure.

What hurt him most was that the Catholic Church, which he had aways tried to protect from the vicious attacks by the Nazis, abandoned him and his fellow Center Party members. The Church was so eager to please the Nazis that his friend and mentor, Prelate Ernst Foehr, the Church's official delegate to Government institutions, dropped him like a hot potato after Hitler had signed the infamous Concordat, the 'peace' treaty with the Vatican. Under this diabolic pact the Church agreed not speak up against the Hitler regime in exchange for the 'protection' of the Church's clergy and its properties. Like any other agreement with Hitler it would only last as long as it would suit him and his henchmen. Ernst Foehr succeeded in saving his own skin for a while, but it did not take long for the Nazis to start persecute him, too.

We will never run out of bad things to say about the Nazis, but perhaps one could give them a grudging bit of credit for always being consistent and absolutely transparent about their plans. Unlike most politicians who promise one thing and then, once in power do something else, the Nazis carried out exactly what they had said they would do: they put everyone who would oppose them in jail, cruelly persecute Jews, gypsies, homosexuals, intellectuals, and anyone else they decided not to like, and then they started World War II, mainly to grab land for their so-called "Master Race." Throughout these times, average Germans found themselves wishing that the Nazis had been as dishonest about their aims as most politicians and would go back to 'business as usual' once they had succeeded in securing power.

You see, most Germans expected this to happen with the Nazis and many were sorely disappointed that the Nazis turned out to be true to their word in being every bit as evil and ruthless as they said they would be. To everybody's horror and surprise, the Nazis found seemingly limitless ways to use terror to stay in power. Much to German people's lasting disgrace, altogether too many Germans tacitly supported the Nazis' madness when it was still time to resist, fearful for their own lives and the lives of their loved ones.

It was Mama who always came through as a pillar of quiet strength holding the family together while we were all being pulled in different directions by our increasingly dangerous and hostile environment. The strength of character needed to cope with so much unaccustomed adversity came from my parents' solid upbringing, and from generations of their ancestors who had shown them how to ultimately prevail in the most trying of situations.

Our extended family was solidly in Father's court, except for Mama's older brother Hermann. A much decorated WWI hero, he had survived a shot in his head and lost one eye. I remember him fondly for his inexhaustible supply of jokes, some not fit for polite society, which endeared him much to us youngsters. Like Father, he was in the highly regarded German Civil Service. Cutting a dashing figure as a Lieutenant in the Kaiser's Army, he moved in 'higher circles' and married a girl from the local nobility. His wife was ambitious, and following the fashionable trend, she became a rabid Nazi. Rumors had it that she had developed a rather cozy relationship with the Baden State's notorious Governor Wagner and thereby managed to catapult her husband to become his right-hand man. In his position of power, Onkel Hermann offered to help Father re-enter his career, but only if Father would agree to become a member of the Nazi party. This, of course, he refused to do.

Though beleaguered from all sides, he would not budge. His friends would lean on him: "Come on now, don't be so stubborn. It's the new way of things, just make some allowances and swallow your pride. Get with it whether you like the bastards or not - they are the new reality!"

Mama would say: "I know you are hurting terribly. What they have done to you is awful. But we have to live, and as long as you oppose them you will not be allowed to work. Like it or not, think of your family!"

Brothers Hermann and Waldemar, in their teens and starting in Gymnasium were worried, too:"Papa, please do something. Already we are not allowed to play soccer with them. They will expel us, and then what? How can you kill our chances! We won't be able to go to university! And why not join our German renewal? What's so difficult about being a good German?"

Anneliese and I were too young then to understand all of this. We were lovingly shielded by Mama and Papa from their fears and their suffering. But nothing could keep us from listening to their arguments through closed doors.

Well, Father was stubborn. He had an unshakable faith in the basic decency of the German people and felt sure that the country would not stand for all this Nazi nonsense for long. And his final words in all these heated arguments were "if more of you would speak out against this abomination we would be able to change it." But many Germans would not heed his words. Too many were betting on the Hitler regime being as short-lived as all the other political coalitions in the years before. They were terribly wrong: Not only did the Nazis stay in power, but they got a lot worse. And, sure enough, when the time came for Hermann and Waldemar to apply for university, they were told not to waste their time. No way would they be admitted with an 'Un-German' father like that. The fact that by that time they had done their compulsory military service did not mean anything. But then the war would come and change everything.

In the meantime there would be the usual family visits with much good-natured bantering - but those with Onkel Hermann's family were stressful to say the least. The rare visits with them would always end up in bitter arguments, mostly about why Father would not join the Nazi party and why he would continue in his vocal criticism of the Nazi's ever tightening oppression. Often I saw Onkel Hermann's wife storming out of the room hysterically threatening to tell the police or even the Governor. Somehow, Onkel Hermann always succeeded in smoothing things over, at least to the extent that his wife would not denounce us as "enemies of the people." These were close calls, though. Like so many families, ours also wound up deeply divided, certainly with Onkel Hermann's. It took a lot of effort not to let these rifts become lethal.

After the war had ended, his wife and oldest daughter Hanna committed suicide, having been brutally abused by a mob bent on revenge. Although never accused of any war crimes, Onkel Hermann was put into prison for having served in a high position in the Nazi administration. Through his connections with the French military government, Father succeeded in easing his prison conditions and he got him an early release. When asked why he would help Onkel Hermann after having gotten no help from him in his own time of distress, Father would say "just because somebody has failed me is no reason for me to fail him in his time of need."

Now that is Character.

Character resists expedience. It is deeply engrained, etched into a person's integrity. My father's strength of convictions determined my own for the rest of my life.

My admiration for character had another side of the coin: my vulnerability to people of ill intent. That, as it turned out, would become a problem in my life. It made me weak in the face of duplicity and deceit, because I would expect truthfulness that comes with character.

In the absence of character, there is no truthfulness.

Onkel Hermann would re-marry a Berlin woman who tried her best to fit in with the rest of our very Southern German family, but rubbed us the wrong way with her all-too 'Prussian' brittleness that often came across as unloving, harsh, and conceited. They settled in a very nice condo near the beautiful spa town Baden-Baden, giving us many occasions for joyous

family visits in this lovely setting, with great dinners, like in the fabulously elegant Europaeischer Hof, or in the picture-book vineyards of Neuweier. Mama and Father had reconciled with Onkel Hermann, but not quite fully, and there always remained a small dose of chilly reserve. I would routinely stop at their place for some libation during my student years, on my way back from Karlsruhe University to Gengenbach. Onkel Hermann's younger daughter Inge became my good friend and consoled me when I was down from too much hard studying, and like a good cousin gave me female company away from my studies. She would marry an executive with Daimler Benz whose brusk manners made nobody happy. Onkel Hermann died at a ripe old age, commiserating often with Father about not having the pleasure to see grandchildren in their lifetime.

Family is our most basic social institution and the source of our strength. Keep the family together even when the past brings a lot of heavy baggage.

But the Nazis had succeeded in sowing mistrust into almost all families, and we learned to be careful and to fend for ourselves as best we could. Survival was the issue. True, too many Germans at that time made compromises that in hindsight seem dreadfully wrong. It's easy to judge them now, but only when you are in the middle of oppression and aware of the dire consequences for yourself and your wife and your children can you truly understand. Especially after the war had started, we would hear more and more often about people being detained for the most trivial reasons - for cracking a joke about the lack of food, or about some Nazi official that had made a fool of himself. And then, the whispered news of someone in our neighborhood having disappeared. You had to be very careful indeed.

Yet there were enduring friendships. Like with our neighbors around the corner, the Principal of the elementary school, a burly man who was all authority, at least in our eyes. He was a highly decorated veteran of the first world war, in which he had lost his right arm. Their two daughters were in Gymnasium with my sister and me, but a bit older. Our parents knew each other also from church, and they gradually developed enough confidence in each other to talk about all kind of matters that usually are only covered among friends. Our 'Victory Garden' backed up to theirs, and eventually we would go together foraging for some extra food in the country-side. But most of the time, we cautiously kept apart, like everybody else, not willing to risk a breach of trust.

Once we were invited into their home for a birthday party!

A party! A break from the dreary everyday fight for food, the never ending air raid drills, the Nazi 'Information Meetings.' Even I, writing about this seemingly little event some seventy years later, have a hard time recalling how much such a small social gathering had meant to us. How can anyone possibly understand who has not lived through periods like these?

For us at that time, it was a wondrous break in our dark war days. We were happy with any little thing that would bring us a light moment. Perhaps there would even be a small cake, a little juice, and for our parents perhaps a cup of 'Ersatz' coffee. We knew not to expect anything more. We, like they, had little to spare, but it didn't matter. We excitedly rehearsed the little poem we wanted to recite as our birthday present.

I still remember how they had decorated their home. Flowers everywhere, the table set with their fine china, an embroidered tablecloth and matching napkins - the 'gemuetlich' German middle class setting just as it should be. We sang, we recited poems, we drank, and we ate the delicious cake. Her father broke out the brandy he had saved for this occasion. Warm happiness all around.

Then the birthday girl stood up. Glowing with pride, she announced to her parents that she had signed up to join the 'Lebensborn' to have a baby for her Fuehrer and the Vaterland.

For a moment there was stunned silence. It was as though we were frozen in our chairs. Her father glared at her trying to understand. "What did you say?" was all he could get out. Again: "What did you say?"

Not quite so sure of herself any more she said "well, now that I am eighteen, I am able to do my duty to my country."

Her father and mother looked at each other in disbelief. Then all hell broke loose. Her mother cried hysterically, her father, red in the face, thundered "how could you do such a thing - are you out of your mind? "

He could not believe it. Here stood his daughter, in his eyes still his sweet little girl, in her youthful determination to do what her Group Leader had put into her head: "You are to have a baby for your country from a true Arian!"

Her father would not have any of this. No way. "You go right now and tell your Leader that you are not going to do this, no way!"

Defiant, looking her father straight into the eye she yelled: "Nobody, not you, not anybody, will keep me from doing my duty! And I will tell my Leader what you said!" At that, everybody fell silent. Would she really denounce her parents? So may others had done this awful thing. Even my sister and I, then only 13 and 14 years old, knew what that meant - interrogations, stern warnings at best, and most likely a lot worse. Marked an 'Enemy of the Vaterland' her father would be removed from his position, and then what?

The party was over. My father shook his friend's hand and looking into his eyes for a long moment, signaling his full support, as mother gave her sobbing friend a warm embrace. There was nothing else we could do.

In their unfathomable immorality the Nazis had created this 'Lebensborn' in the middle of WWII in response to Germany's staggering human losses. It was an institution where soldiers meeting the Nazi criteria of the 'Master Race' would be invited to impregnate young girls. Their babies would be given up to special orphanages to be raised to become good Nazis - and cannon fodder for future wars - a flagrant case of the State imposing its morbid concept of morality on brain-washed young people who simply no longer knew better.

Fortunately, what could have been an absolute horror ended well enough. She rescinded her decision to enter the 'Lebensborn,' under the excuse of citing her commitment to nursing convalescent soldiers in the nearby military hospital. No doubt, her family's solid morality came through. Surely it also helped that she saw the same convictions in her neighbors. Contrary to what the rest of the world had thought at that time, not all Germans had lost their moral compass.

The Family Mack

In Times of Test, Family is Best - Burmese Proverb

Home, sweet home, was the refuge from chaos, our little heaven in a world that was becoming increasingly a heartless one. But inside was comfort, security, and cooperation. We knew we could rely on each other no matter what. And compared with the rest of the people we knew, we felt we were well off, even though money was often scarce.

Before the Nazis had devastated our family's economic status, we always had live-in servants, at least until our 'circumstances were reduced.' Then we had day-help only, diminishing in frequency as we, the young ones, left home. Our live-in helpers were not 'professionals', they were usually simple girls from farms. In return for doing much of the house work they were taught household skills and manners, how to take care of children, to make them better prepared for life when they got married. This was a well-established and quite useful way to give those girls a much needed education while they were helping families like ours with their work load.

Mama was very good at all of that, and because of her training in home economics, she would systematically and patiently teach them to cook nutritious meals to augment their often one-sided diets. When they would taste meals that were new to them, Mama would ask them how they liked it, and, of course, they did. Their standard answer, however, would be, in their heavy Alemanic dialect, something like "ma chaas aesse," meaning "yes, one can eat it." For them, that would be the best compliment they were able to give, even though outsiders could interpret it as rude. It became one of our family's inside jokes. Several of these girls kept in close touch with us in their later lives when they had families of their own, thankful for what Mama had taught them.

We children were always told to work alongside them and to never place any extra demands on them. We especially were admonished to respect them like members of our family, and to keep our own rooms clean and to always pick up after ourselves. It showed us children that acceptance of others did not depend on their backgrounds, but on their and our will to work and live together in mutual respect.

Rules to live by were simple: take care of your body, your things, keep order and be clean. Clean up you own messes. Flush. Do not be a burden to any one. Do your fair share of chores. Do your home work. Make good behavior your natural routine to make your social life easier:

"Behave at home as if you were with the King - then, when you are with the King, you can behave like being at home".

Don't procrastinate - things not done will pile up and clutter up your brain. Above all, don't lie - it destroys trust, and after a while you yourself will lose the understanding what is real and what is not. And never, ever, fake sickness when in reality all you want is to shirk your duties. Before you will be conscious of it, your faked illnesses may become a

reality.

And always keep busy - no room for boredom, with lots of reading. Hands-on activities like gardening, model building and long bicycle rides through the countryside were my preferences. For my meticulous replica of a Viking ship I would get a school prize (at age 12 - no pre-manufactured parts then, everything from scratch!).

Was our upbringing ideal? Of course not. Certainly there were parts that could or should have been done better, even in the context of the times. For one, the emphasis on honesty at all cost probably caused me some difficulties later on in life, as did the almost unyielding faith in, and unconditional believe in justice. In the real world, you cannot expect that everything and everybody will deal with you justly. To rely on this laudable but sometimes impractical mindset can be frustrating and damaging to one's career and social life, and one's blood pressure. Perhaps it would have been better had our parents modified their edicts on unconditional truthfulness, for example by adding that you must be prepared that some people will lie with great skill, and you have to know how to deal with their conniving. Sure, you always have to tell the truth, *but you do not always have to speak out everything that is true*.

Small incidents became 'teaching moments.' I was perhaps five when Mama started to send me for groceries to our neighborhood store. One of these little missions included getting a re-fill of our bottle of Maggi, the quintessential European cooking flavoring. I liked Maggi a lot (I still do), and on the way home from the grocer I would take a few good sips. Mama saw that the newly refilled bottle was not quite full to the top and she started to blame the grocer for trying to short-change us, threatening to take her business elsewhere. Now I was on the spot. Admitting my doing most likely would get me into trouble. Not saying anything would unjustly penalize the friendly grocer. I agonized for a few days until I finally decided to tell my mother about my skimming. Mama did the right thing. It was okay to skim, but to get somebody else in trouble by being dishonest was really the bad thing. For that, not for the skimming, I was given a few slaps on my behind, just enough to reinforce the point.

In the more intimate issues of growing up, Father was ever the realist. There would be no big moralizing sermons but lots of brief statements of facts with no dwelling on details. After that we just would go on with the task of everyday living. Mama, by contrast, was always ready for teaching moments. She also had no interest in moralizing. Whenever we would come to her with our probing questions, or when she discovered tell-tale signs of our youthful indiscretions, her typical comment would be "this is natural." It was great to grow up without the guilt implanted in so many other young people in those days. These were good lessons by our parents on the right subjects in the right connotation.

To the outside world, Father appeared reserved, and as a part of his position of authority (as little as it really was) he perhaps also acted out the 'person of importance' syndrome with his air of gravitas and upright dignity that in those days were mostly defensive, to keep his hierarchical distance. Those who were close to him knew that he was really quite soft in many ways, and certainly enjoyed a good joke. One of his favorites:

The old spinster was publicly castigating the town's drunkard for having spent yet another night in the neighborhood bar. "How do you know that I was drinking?" he asked her. "Well, it was obvious what you were doing in there- your car was parked in front of the bar" she said with a sneer. The next night he parked his car in front of the spinster's house, for everybody to see...

Our religious life had changed. Throughout the Nazi terror and the Germany's wars of aggression the Church acted pretty much as nothing was happening. We had always loved the Church's basic teachings, its cultural, spiritual and social aspects and its uplifting music and pageantry. As expected, I was an altar boy, and my family had their special pew right next to the altar.

Faced with the very increasing oppression by the Nazi regime, many Germans were looking for political and emotional help from the nation's institutions and, of course, from their religions. The first to disappoint the Germans in this search was the judiciary - it had sold itself out to the Nazis, just to be sure that they would keep their jobs. Then we were looking to our military, traditionally an 'unpolitical' force claiming for themselves the highest standards of patriotism and honor. The military was dominated by the sons of the German aristocracy, who in addition to their position of power also had a high degree of financial independence - most of them came from the rich landowner class. To Germany's terrible disappointment these men turned out to be the worst cowards when confronted with the bullying by Hitler and the other Nazi goons.

That left the religious institutions. With very few exceptions, they, too, failed their flock. We had witnessed the Church's reprehensible complicity with the Nazis, when saving its own position became more important to them than protecting its flock. After all, the Vatican had made an odious agreement with Hitler, the infamous Concordat, by which the Church consented to stay quiet in exchange for the safety of its clergy and its property. The Church had found it much more important to insist on doctrine and dogma than speaking out against the actual evil in the real world. We believed that there were much more pressing problems than doctrines, like why eating meat on Fridays would land us in hell (most of the time there was no meat to eat anyway).

In the rare instances when the Church did speak up against the Nazis it was mostly when church property was being confiscated, like the monasteries and convents whose great land holdings were often converted to Nazi boarding schools and para-military training grounds. I vividly remember a sermon by Monsignor Feuerstein of Donaueschingen that landed him in a concentration camp. His protest was not directed at the Nazis' war crimes, the barbaric prosecution of the Jews but instead he protested the confiscation of the church bells (for the metal). In a scathing attack on the notorious Nazi Minister of Propaganda Goebbels, who just before had told the Germans that "the bells of peace would soon be heard ringing" the Monsignor thundered: "You are wrong, these bells will obviously not be around anymore to announce peace". As emotionally difficult as the taking of the church bells was for the townspeople, it seemed to us that this was a small matter compared to the enormous Nazi crimes. Obviously, something was awfully wrong with the Church's priorities. Most of us simply walked away from the Church as an institution that could have been such a great source of consolation and moral leadership when it was needed so badly.

By its own intransigence, and by its failure to confront the Nazi terror, the Church as an organization lost much of its credibility. In the eyes of its flock, the Church's actions were in stark contradiction of its teachings of christian love and charity. No wonder that so many European catholics turned away from the Church, even in traditionally strong catholic countries like Italy and Spain. In America, where people had not experienced the realities caused by war and the Church's complicity with oppressors, catholics would continue in their unshakeable faith in the Church as an institution, as I would discover to my astonishment when I came to America in the mid-fifties. But even here, it would catch up a few decades later, when the Church had 'painted itself into a corner' with its unenforceable edicts on divorce, birth control and interfaith marriages. Also, I was perplexed at the American catholic's initial disbelief of the rampant abuse of children by priests. In Europe this had been common knowledge all along - we alter boys were told by our parents to be careful and "never be alone with the priests."

In the end, stripped of a lot of useless trappings, our religious life became more deeply spiritual, looking to its uplifting elements, and simply living by the Golden Rule:

"Do unto others as you want them to do unto you."

Our family stayed spiritually intact, with its down-to-earth morality.

<O>

On the Mack Farms

*"A human life should well be rooted in some spot of native land,
where it may get the kinship for the face of the earth"* (George Eliot)

Even with our fair share of troubles we lived the life of a typical urban family, first in pleasant old Gengenbach, and then in the state capital Karlsruhe. It is the seat of the university where many years later I was to study engineering. Karlsruhe offered lots of cultural events which Father and Mama would take in whenever they could. We certainly looked at ourselves as city people. However Father made sure that that our young lives also took us to the farming country of his youth.

The small, ancient farming town of Rohrbach became my second home town. Set in the lovely bucolic rolling hills of the Kraichgau, just south of Heidelberg, it had some of the most fertile farm lands of Southwest Germany. 'Rohrbach' means 'reed creek', and as there are other farm towns established around similar creeks, there are quite a few "Rohrbachs" in that part of Germany. 'My' Rohrbach is the the one near Eppingen. Here Father was born, in 1884, the youngest child of eight, into a family of modestly prosperous farmers and craftsmen. As it was the custom then, being the youngest, he was given some higher education allowing him to pursue a distinguished career in Germany's prestigious Civil Service, albeit the lower one, the only one open to him with his level of schooling.

Father had made it a point to always maintain close relationships with his hometown relatives. He wanted to make sure we would learn where food comes from and how hard the farmers had to work for it. The few small pieces of land that he had inherited he turned over to his nephews for use (we would call all grown-up relatives uncle and aunt), with the understanding that instead of money they were to pay for the use of the land with the products of their farming. When he made this decision he had no idea that much later it would save us from starvation - once war came with its deprivations, no amount of money would have fed us.

To underline his attachment to Rohrbach, my brothers and I (and sometimes also sister Anneliese) were to spend our Summer and Fall vacations working alongside our Rohrbach relatives, so we would get an understanding of their lives, their work, their farming. Also, living with farm animals was a convenient way to teach us about the basic facts of life. And above all, we had our (second) cousins, lots of them, and most our age, to share work and fun.

Farm towns in Germany's southwest were compact, each farm house sharing the side walls with the neighbor, both for safety and to keep everything in walking distance. Remember, there were few cars then in rural Germany, and each town was surrounded by miles of fields. This closeness, of course, also made for lots of petty jealousies. I would cringe when I had to listen to their often unkind gossip.

My father's family home, typical of homes of other well-off farmers and craftsmen, was solidly built of cut limestone, and was quite spacious. The front door led into a yard with stables, barn, equipment sheds and work shops and then onto a large garden, a favorite place for us children. Self-contained and real family homesteads, they were built to last. After more than 150 years, they still are the homes of my relatives, modernized after multiple renovations, underlining solid continuity.

In order to get out to the fields, you rode on a cart drawn by horses (later in the war by cows), often for an hour or so. Over generations, their land had been divided into smaller and smaller parcels by multiple inheritance. Most farmers wound up with dozens of fields in different spots. This was Napoleon's legacy, who in his days tried to stem the flow of poor, disenfranchised French youngsters from their farms into the city slums, an early example of 'social engineering.' But these long cart rides provided a time for conversation, my uncles and aunts telling me stories, explaining the various crops, saying a short prayer as we passed the little field chapels (having a very practical reason as shelters from inclement weather).

But as a result of this fragmentation much time was lost just getting from one field to another, which made this sort of farming highly inefficient. Later, after the war, this was remedied by a sweeping consolidation of the fields into much larger lots. The soil was good, the quality of the crops excellent, but no matter how hard they tried, farmers never seemed able to produce enough for the growing number of city dwellers. The resulting high food prices and severe wartime shortages posed a perpetual problem. One of Germany's leading agronomists, Prof. Herbert Backe, saw this very clearly, and in his epoch-making book how to make Germany self-sufficient in food production ("Um die Nahrungsfreiheit Europas") he proposed larger, mechanized US-style farms - and massive fertilization.

This resonated well with the Germans. They remembered too well the years of awful starvation during and after the first World War, and they naturally were very eager to find ways to avoid a repetition of that catastrophe. One way was to greatly increase the use of fertilizers - there was not anywhere near enough natural animal dung available. So Germany turned to 'synthetic' fertilizers for which one of the basic production technologies had been developed - surprise - by Prof. Fritz Haber of the Karlsruhe university! Without his nitrogen fixation process, much of the world's population would starve to death.

Backe was a real visionary, and his recommendations to reform German farming were finally put into practice after the war, along with sweeping farm land consolidations. Under the Nazis he served for a while as Agriculture Minister, but Hitler did not like Backe's 'pedestrian' views and decided instead to 'solve' Germany's food problem by conquering Russia, with historically disastrous results. Backe continued in Hitler's service and was put into prison after the war for his role in using forced labor to keep German domestic farming going. After all, most agriculture in Europe was hugely dependent on manual labor at that time.

In my Rohrbach years we, of course, had all the typical rudimentary farm machines, very efficient plows, seeding and soil conditioning equipment, and basic harvesters, but still much was done by very hard physical work.

Onkel Heinrich had horses, and for the more demanding tasks, like on threshing day, he would rent the community 'bulldog' tractor. It was a marvel of simplistic diesel technology, just right for the purpose and the time: no electrics at all, a 'glow bulb' for ignition, and a very simple fuel pump injecting unrefined crude oil into a big slow moving piston. Most repairs could be done by the town blacksmith. Except for its low fuel efficiency it was a very useful design that would do well even now in developing countries.

As the war dragged on, the German army had started to requisition farm horses (believe it or not, horses were still used to pull military supply wagons!). One last ride for us on Onkel Heinrich's fine horses, and then he had to use some

of his cows to pull his wagons! It slowed everything down, but above all, it hurt his pride - only poor farmers used cows for traction. Now the cows were not just there to give milk and bear calves but had to pull the wagons, the plows and the harvesters. No wonder Germans invented the 'Sauerbraten' - in order to make this tough cow meat edible you had to marinate it in vinegar.

Bottom line was that the Rohrbach 'model' may have been good for self-sufficient, well fed, healthy and solid families, but not for mass production of food. Little cash was generated, but theirs was not a money-based economy. Of course, they would have liked to have more money, for example for getting running water instead of the kitchen sink hand pump. Their money needs were for farm equipment, for clothes and for their daughters' dowries. The concept of accumulating money for retirement was foreign to them, and the German social security system already then provided for basic health care and old age benefits.

All this would change dramatically in the years after the war. Today, there is little left of the old farm town atmosphere. Rohrbach is now more like a suburb with only few but much larger farms left, the lovely creek put underground. Today, cousin Friedhelm is gaining weight sitting in his air conditioned combine, playing tennis for exercise, and going to Italy for vacations. Are they happier, or healthier, than their forefathers with their sixteen hour work days?

Nostalgia or not, I did not always like the work, the summer heat, the cold wet earth in autumn and the sometimes scary situations with horses and cows, or farm machinery. But it was extremely valuable training on a very basic level. One other thing that became etched into my mind was their quiet pride in land ownership, as small as their holdings may have been. And they were not about to blame others, or even God, when their hard work was in vain because of weather or blights. They took responsibility, and when they could not influence the outcome, they simply tried again. They did not have much choice either.

While they did not have much money they perfectly understood that they would always have food and shelter, even when their enormous work load would get them down. They were thus largely independent from the many political and economic upheavals of wars, depressions and hyperinflation that would wipe out the economic base for most people, as it had done to us. This was very real because when Father lost his job and was forbidden to make a living in his profession, the little land he had inherited was a true lifesaver for us. All this was driven home to me by watching my Rohrbach families holding up throughout the turmoil of war and depression, like Onkel Josef's that would host me quite a few times. Ownership of land is the best guaranty for survival and for solid prosperity.

Onkel Josef was a pillar of strength, and ruled rambunctious family with a firm, sometimes autocratic hand. He would later become Burgermeister of Rohrbach. He was a strong leader in a very small community who like so many upright Germans worked hard to bring Germany back from so many years of war and the horrific crimes of the Nazis.

Did any of these exposures to the hard life of our farming relatives pay off for me, and did I make meaningful contributions to their often back-breaking work? I like to think so. I did not want them to think of me as a pampered city kid, and because of that (and because my parents told me to do real

work there)I made every effort to prove myself. But I also knew (and that is even more clear to me now) that they often indulged me, as a part of their admiration for my father's position which, in their minds, was something elevated and honorable. The little land we owned put me in a somewhat different category from the other city kids relocated to country towns like Rohrbach during and after the war. I saw that they had to beg for extra food to take home to their parents, while I was given this extra food because our relatives felt it was our proper due.

There was an element of entitlement that, in a way, prevented me later on from learning to negotiate from a position of relative weakness, and this would accompany me for the rest of my life. That was actually not one of my better lessons.

But there were many more episodes to teach me important positive life lessons. Like obedience. One rainy day, cousin Paul and I were playing way up in his father's barn instead of doing the chores requested by his mother, Tante Berta. Justifiably, she became quite upset, telling Onkel Josef, who then climbed up the barn ladder after us to set us straight. Having caught up with us, he just said, "Look, you really must cooperate if you want to be with us." I was ashamed and impressed with his self-control and his ability to keep things in perspective. Going back down the ladder he slipped, fell and broke several ribs. Right or wrong, I felt responsible for his mishap, and the feeling of guilt was a powerful learning experience.

Also, I learned the importance of telling the truth. One day, I was told to bring the bread dough to Onkel Eiermann's community bakery. The dough had been put into rather large woven straw baskets and these were loaded into a small hand drawn cart (a 'Leiterwaegele' in the local dialect) for transfer to the bakery, a few hundred yards down the unpaved street. I became a bit careless, and playing around with the little cart it turned over, the bread dough spilling all over the road. Looking around to make sure nobody would see, I quickly scraped the dough from the road, put it back into the baskets, and went off to have the bread baked. The next day, at lunch, Tante Berta cut the first of the big loaves, after making the traditional sign of the cross over its back. My uncle, being served first, bit into it, to find gravel and sand. I cringed. What to do: should I let my poor aunt take the blame, or should I tell the truth? Well, I decided to tell the truth, expecting the worst. First they all sat there in stoney silence. And then they all broke out in uproarious laughter, except for Tante Berta who knew how much good flour and work was wasted, and who had to do the bread dough routine all over again.

By the way, 'Leiterwaegele' were great for racing down the hills, steering pole between our legs, the inevitable and often spectacular crashes being the best part.

Father arranged it that we would stay with different relatives so that we would get to understand how different families arranged their lives, their habits and their demands. But mostly I stayed with Onkel Heinrich and Tante Emilie. He was witty and had a great sense of self-deprecating humor. One of his favorite stories was this:

There was this farmer who would complain about everything: too much rain, too little rain, too many mice, and on and on. Then, one year, everything went well, with a once-in-a-life-time bumper crop. Everyone was elated, his friends teasing him:"This year for sure you have nothing to complain about!" His downcast answer:"Yeah, but how this depleted my soil!"

Tante Emilie was very good to me, but also, gently but surely, they demanded no less than my full and active help. That meant quite hard work, in the fields, cleaning the stables, feeding the cows and pigs. I liked working around the animals, especially their huge black Belgian horse. To be allowed to ride the horse to the fields was heaven. On Saturday evenings, after a week's worth of hard work, we would ride the horses into the Rohrbach creek, then running open through the town, to wash off the worst of their sweat and dust. This was great fun, and I quickly learned to jump off before the horse would decided to roll over in the water to cool off.

One of my many chores was getting lunch to the field workers, including big crocks of hard cider, of which I would take more than just a little taste, especially on hot days. Little did I know that my less than steady walk and my overpowering sleepiness always would give me away. Onkel Heinrich and Tante Emilie, cousins Reinhold and Friedhelm and everybody else in sight would grin at each other from ear to ear.

And the things I liked least: going into the dark root cellar to sort out last year's sprouting potatoes, some of them rotting and full of creepy crawlers. When I would show my disgust with this and some other less pleasant tasks, Onkel Heinrich or Tante Emilie simply said that "somebody has to do it, if you want us to do it instead, okay, but when mealtime comes around, just think about it…"

Another dreaded task was scraping the mud and accumulated animal dung from the street in front of the farm house every Saturday evening. The street 'pavement' was made of tightly compacted crushed limestone from local quarries. The steel-rimmed farm carts would gradually grind the limestone into fine dust, turning it into a glob of mud and animal scat. Using a special broad hoe the scrapings had to be dumped onto the farm's dung heap. It made for good fertilizer and soil conditioner, but not the most pleasant of tasks!

One day we went out to harvest a field of wheat, a very large field by any standard. I might have been about ten or eleven. It was beastly hot, and all of us looked in awe at the size of the field, trying to muster the courage to tackle this enormous job that we knew would last all day and well into the sweltering summer night. Tante Emilie saw how much I dreaded a long day in the summer heat. Actually, my task was an easy one, laying out the ties for the bundling of harvester-cut sheaths of wheat. It looked simple enough, but you had to lay these ties down at just the right place and in the right distance from each other to match up with the piles of mowed wheat. If I didn't do it right, it would upset the routine of the men coming through to compress the piles and tie them into solid bundles for easy handling afterwards. Even such a simple job required full attention and and some form of basic skill. It gave me a deep respect for anyone who acquired a skill, any skill, and applied it to make an honest living.

Tante Emilie did not excuse me from my job but to make the day easier for me she told me to take the workers' food and drink into a nearby shady cavern to keep it fresh in the cool stream running through it. It would be my job, in addition to the regular one, to bring food and drink to anyone who needed it. Well, that was pretty much the best job for that hot day: I very happily went to that cool place anytime somebody asked for a drink…and I 'tasted' the hard cider on every one of my many trips there. Her concern for the limits of a little boy's stamina made me grateful to her forever. But she also made it clear to me that she expected me never to shy away from hard work. In her direct and simple way, she told me that would be just be letting myself down, as well as failing everybody around me, too.

Favorite hang-outs were Merkel's store - one of those country stores that would carry just about everything useful to the farmers' wives. Also, there was Onkel Eiermann's bakery where on Sundays after Mass, Tante Lina and Onkel Alois would treat me to an extra-large scoop of their incomparable home-made ice cream, while the older ones quenched their thirst with local Jehle beer in the Loewen pub next door. Sundays were deliciously slow and leisurely, truly days of carefree rest, among the fondest of memories of a time long gone.

On sweltering summer days, cousin Paul and I and a few of our buddies would dam up the creek to make a little swimming hole. The miller downstream would come running, steaming mad and tearing down our dam to undo the temporary loss of water for his water wheel. Nothing I said could convince him that, if he would wait just a few more minutes, the water would flow over our little dam at exactly the same rate as it flowed before.

It is difficult to imagine more formative summers. Today, we have organized summer camps for the kids while the parents are off doing their own things. We had truly working summer 'vacations.' Certainly, I learned first hand the enormous amount of work and coordination it takes to produce food. People today would do well to spend a little time working on a farm. Knowledge of what's really involved might change frivolous attitudes in our dubious relationship to food. Those of us who have lived through the agonies of hunger know the truth - without large-scale mechanized farming and intensive fertilizer use we would all have starved to death a long time ago.

<O>

Phases of our Lives

A Boy at War

"War is Hell" - William Tecumseh Sherman

Phases of our Lives

What War does to a Family

War did not spare our family. Every war is insanity, especially when started frivolously. And those who start a war always say that it was the other side that's to blame. It reminds me of what our four sons would say when they had their occasional fights. When I asked them how it had started they invariably would say "it all started when he hit me back..."

That was certainly so with World War II. The Nazis had forged an unholy alliance with big industry, promising huge and lucrative armament contracts. The ultra right-wing land barons were intent on amassing ever larger land holdings, and cheered the Nazi plan of taking land from neighboring Poland.

The war also gave the Nazis justification to crush the internal opposition which was growing in response to the Nazis' ever more oppressive dictatorship. Just like warmongers anywhere, they sold their war to the Germans as a somehow noble cause forced upon them by our evil neighbors. Of course, for the Nazis it was all about power, glory - and plunder. And as always, it would be the fathers, the mothers and the children everywhere who would carry the awful burdens of war. As it turned out, our family would have to shoulder more than

our fair share of it.

Let's start with stories about my brothers. Hermann, twelve years older, had not liked the military, and certainly had no desire to be in the war - it prevented him from going on to university and living the life he wanted. He had learned from father how despicable the Nazis were, but the truth is that Hermann was not

 entirely immune to the trappings of his rising position in the army. He cherished riding next to the commander at the head of his unit of foot soldiers (yes, until the middle of the World War, German army officers still were

riding on horse back in front of their soldiers!). In the summer of 1942 his unit headed to the Eastern front, the prospect of which struck fear into the hardest heart. But we were hopeful - just weeks before, he had been assigned to divisional headquarters to serve as deployment officer. The higher-ups had seen that he was an excellent planner. We thought this might keep him from the worst fighting, in their advance to what we only learned later would be the battle of Stalingrad. Our hopes were dashed cruelly later that summer when we learned that had been "killed in action".

Terribly frightened, Anneliese and I clung to each other, while Mama sobbed uncontrollably, and Father screamed out his pain. His oldest son, with so much promise, was now dead because an irresponsible madman had plunged Germany into an absolutely insane war. Father had been seething with disgust inside all along at the Nazis' deceits and ruthlessness, but now he was all fury, and he wasn't careful about who knew it. His open show of hatred of the Nazi regime would have been enough to land him in concentration camp had it not been for the local Nazi administrators who, for once, showed forbearance out of respect for our loss. In some of them, at least, their humanity was not entirely lost yet.

I was twelve at that time, and was too stunned to know how to deal with the loss of my brother. Hermann was twenty four at his death, double my age then. He was the quintessential older brother, who I looked up to as my role model, my confidant, and as a source of pride when he would come home on leave and I could show him off to my schoolmates. He was strong in every sense, serious in everything he did, in school, in sports, in his friendships. Much to my regret, he never bragged about any of his exploits in athletics, especially in swimming - he was the one who taught me. He also was an excellent horseman (I still have a trophy from one of his jumping competitions). And he wouldn't talk about his experiences as a soldier. But his quiet self-assurance left no doubt about his leadership qualities. You could see that he would have a great future, one day with a fine family and an enviable career. Now all that was lost forever.

Brother Waldemar was different. He was older than I by ten years, but was much more of a buddy to me. He was lots of fun to be with, irreverent and ready to laugh and joke in every situation. His astute mind readily saw through the lies and hypocrisies of the Nazis, and he was a master at poking not so gentle fun at everybody and everything. Anneliese and I loved him for his quick wit, but Father, much more serious in nature, did not appreciate it at all. He would often scold him for not doing better at school and became

furious with him every time he would receive a reprimand from his teachers for 'lack of respect' and 'challenging their authority.' But that is what I loved most about him.

As you would expect, Waldemar truly hated being a soldier, and made no bones about it. Not surprisingly, this got him into trouble in the military. What saved him in these (potentially serious) confrontations was his uncanny ability to see through seemingly complex logistics situations, even under the stress of combat. This made him valuable in the eyes of his commanders, and saved him in his run-ins with the military hierarchy. He would become an expert in field communications, and this probably kept him alive for three horrible years on the Eastern front. He was wounded several times, and we would see him then on his hard-earned furloughs during his recuperations. He had never been physically very strong, and we were amazed that he could handle so much pain and misery. It was clear to see that he was being worn down by a war that he hated with every fiber of his being.

I will never forget when he came down the street on his last unannounced furlough. We were walking back home from church, and he appeared a few blocks up the street, limping slowly, leaning heavily on a cane, his uniform hanging loosely on his emaciated frame. I saw him first and cried out "here is Waldemar, Waldemar is here!" It took a few moments for his own parents to recognize their son. Their boy, so full of joy for life before, now was a broken shell of his former self. To see him sent back to the front soon afterward was an unbearable heartbreak for us all.

At few weeks later, he wrote to us that he was not to go back to the eastern front. His leg injuries were bad enough that he could no longer walk without a cane. In carefully chosen words that only we would be able to understand he let us know that he was now stationed 'near our old home across the river.' That could only mean in nearby France, in Alsace. We were ecstatic at this news. In our wishful thinking, this meant that he would be safe, far away from the hellish eastern front.

That was the last we heard from him. In the chaos of the last months of the war, all communications broke down. There was no notification of his death at all. Not from the military, not from the Red Cross, not from any possible source, not even that he was 'missing.' Just silence. When Hermann's death had been announced to us we are stunned, anguished, and furious, but there was some level of sanity to be found in its clear finality. In the total void of information about Waldemar's fate, our family sank into a state of quiet despair. Like most Germans at that point, we were worn out from over four years of war. So much death, so much misery, so much meaningless destruction. The uncertainty about Waldemar was gnawed at us constantly.

More than a year after the end of the war we found out what happened to him. By then, Father had been reinstated into the positions he had held before the Nazis, and among those was his honorary leadership in the German war cemetery commission. He saw this incredibly sad job as an important and necessary duty that held responsibility for coordination with his French counterparts in nearby Alsace. Sifting through a mountain of personal belongings of the war dead his crew stumbled across Waldemar's identification documents.

Piecing together bits of seemingly unrelated information, it appeared that Waldemar had been declared medically unfit for active duty. But instead of releasing him to go home, he was assigned to a small army field office for processing the repatriation of wounded soldiers. Apparently his small detachment had been overrun by French resistance fighters who had killed everyone in the unit. He was finally put to rest in the sprawling Niederbronn war cemetery, a lasting memorial to the insanity of all wars.

A few years later, Anneliese and I took Mama there. Even then, her grief was almost unbearable for us to witness. I will never forget her saying over and over, looking at the thousands of grave markers:

> *"Every one of these men had mothers and fathers.*
> *They may have come from different walks of life,*
> *but all of them had one thing in common -*
> *not one of them wanted to end up here."*

Again, many years later, we took our son Wolf and his young family there, including their four year old Sophie, our first grandchild. A rotunda-like chapel had been built to commemorate the awful legacy of war. The architects had done something unusual - they had built it with some particular acoustic effects. As we walked in the eerie silence of the chapel, our foot steps reverberated so as to simulate the sound of a distant battle. It was very emotional. Try as I might, I could not keep from sobbing.

That day, there was a group of French high school students in the cemetery doing maintenance chores. I walked over to them and thanked them for doing such a laudable thing. The students told me that all the local communities did this, and that they took it quite seriously indeed. Impressed, I expressed the wish that their German counterparts would do it too. "Oh," they said, "they do! We take care of the German cemeteries, and German students take care of the French and the American ones". This was organized this way for all to remember how tragic and senseless are all wars no matter which side you were fighting for.

Anneliese and I often ask ourselves what our lives would have been like if our brothers had lived, what kind of lives they would have had, what kind of families they would have built, what they would have done with so much promise, ability, and goodness of heart. We have to content ourselves with fond memories of the years when we were all young together. And we can only wish that our sons and grandchildren never have to face such a fate. The sad fact was that Anneliese and I no longer had our brothers. So the two of us would cling together tightly, and from then on were always there for each other in our growing-up years. Our losses would scar us both for life. Every time my wife and I look at our four sons we are happy that they can go through their lives with each other, something that for my sister and I had been taken from us by the madness of war.

<O>

How I saw the War

The war had become a reality for me soon after it started in Autumn of 1939. First experience: the uprooting of the family from our Karlsruhe home.

Only a few miles from the French border, Karlsruhe was in Allied artillery range, and as the capital of the Baden province, an immediate target. Most people deemed necessary for the war effort were immediately evacuated. Our family was moved to the High Black Forest town of Donaueschingen, where Father was put in charge of civilian supplies. His anti-Nazi stance was not forgotten, but the necessities of the war made even the most ardent Nazis bend a little when it suited them.

Donaueschingen was a small but interesting town, known mostly as the source of the mighty Danube river, the longest in Europe. One reason some government departments were relocated there was that the town was about eighty miles from the French border and thus assumed to be safe from war action. It had a good number of comfortable

town residences that were requisitioned to house relocated administrative offices and families. This is how our family wound up with a sizable, comfortable home. The planners had forgotten only one thing - the town's huge army base, its weapons depots, and its outsized rail junction would eventually make it a prime target for air raids.

The town also was the seat of the Fuerstenberg family with their magnificent castle. The presence of the Fuerstenbergs, with their vast land holdings and conservative political clout would become helpful for the townspeople in coping with increasing hardships as the war came closer. It also gave the town a cultural and societal uniqueness that we learned to appreciate. At first, life continued pretty much as before. The war was still a good distance away. But all this would change soon. Few of us had even the remotest notion of the disasters about to engulf us.

For us youngsters, there was the little boys' section of the Hitler Youth movement. At age ten, you were expected to sign up for this Nazi version of the Boy Scouts, fashioned also after the Soviet Komosols with (what else would you expect) German paramilitary programs. We boys liked the camaraderie, the fun-and-games part, the singing around the camp fires. We learned many songs, not just the obligatory Nazi ones, but quite a few good traditional German folk songs. To this day, I occasionally find myself humming or singing some of them.

In theory, there was no actual compulsion to join these youth groups, but not to join would brand you as un-German and most likely exclude you from higher education and a good job afterward. Very few families resisted, and neither did we, but not without bitter arguments with Father who was unrelenting in his hatred of the Nazis. Mama was the realist, and also my older brothers, who did not want to become barred from going to University.

At fourteen, we were inducted into the 'Hitler-Youth', the obligatory paramilitary Nazi youth organization. Before any Nazi brainwashing could take root in me me the war came closer, and we were ordered to spend our time cleaning up after air raids and helping to manage the increasing flood of refugees. Then, at the end of September 1944, we were marched off with thousands of other youngsters and old people (men and women), and told to dig defense trenches. My group was sent to the university city of Freiburg, a two days trek on foot. We started with the traditional zig-zag infantry trenches on the Tuniberg mountain vineyard, working the hills with pick-ax and shovels, ten hours a day, sleeping in barns on hay, with cows and horses. It very soon stopped being fun. We were always cold, wet and hungry. The local vintners hated us for destroying their old vineyards, which had been their livelihood for generations.

Things got even worse when, at the end of October, we were ordered to work on an anti-tank ditch. It would go straight for five miles across the valley, 10 feet deep and 15 feet wide on the top, between the steep hillsides of the Tuniberg and the Black Forest foothills on the on the other end. The ditch was meant to create a barrier against the advancing Allied tanks. Imagine the sheer enormousness of the task, digging this massive trench, all by hand, with only shovels and pickaxes. It was incredibly hard work, knee-deep in mud in the cold Autumn rain. At least the rain mostly kept the Allied fighter planes from strafing us. The ruler-straight trench provided no place to take cover. On clear days, they strafed us with abandon. The killing of our fellow diggers, and the horrifying screaming of the wounded showed us then what war was all about.

And then came my worst nightmare:

On November 27, the day before my fifteenth birthday, the nearby city of Freiburg was just about obliterated by incendiary bombs, and when most of the city had gone up in in flames, another wave dropped explosive bombs to finish the job. The city burned for days, thousands died, untold others were horribly burnt. There was not enough water to douse the flames. Half of all the buildings in the city were totally destroyed, much of the rest suffered enough damage to make them uninhabitable.

Once the fires burned themselves out we were ordered to enter the city to help clear the rubble and to collect the dead for burial. Many of the dead could not be identified, burnt beyond recognition, many were missing and would never be found. For them, funeral services would be held right on the ruins of their homes. There is no way to describe the horror and revulsion of this sordid task. After a few days of working in this inferno most of us youngsters were so sick and exhausted that we were sent home, never to be the same again.

By far the greatest personal shock was the violent death of one of my buddies. We were told to bury some horses killed in the air raid, and while digging a few yards away from me he hit an unexploded shell. He was blown to pieces right in front of me. It became my task to run to town to tell his parents. Yes, I was crying all the way. His mother was sobbing uncontrollably, his father screaming at me "why did you not pick him up" as if I could have done anything about putting him back together again. It could have been me.

In the center of Freiburg only its magnificent cathedral remained standing, not a miracle of divine intervention nor of pin-point bombing as some would come to believe, but just because it would not burn, built entirely of stone, six hundred years earlier. No one had expected that Freiburg would become a target for destruction. As a university town with world renowned hospitals, and no industry, it had no air defense capabilities. Much later, when the Allied air campaign records were opened up, it showed that

"Freiburg was targeted because we had pretty much run out of other sizable towns to destroy".

I had seen a lot more than anybody ever should - the horror of war is still with me. For years, I could not even stand fireworks. Most war movies still make me sick, except the very few which tell it as it really is. I like Remarque's "All Quiet on the Western Front," "Path to Glory," or "A Very Long Engagement." Glorifying anything about war is a crime against all those who have not experienced the awful reality of humans slaughtering one another.

You don't want to forget, and you do become determined to do everything possible to stay out of wars. Unfortunately even the most democratically governed nations have not been able to do this, sometimes because there is aggression from the outside, but just as often because there are politicians whose longing for glory are too big for their conscience.

Phases of our Lives

My own Legacies of War

Traumatic events are a part of everybody's life. Some you can deal with and overcome, some not so well. In the best of cases you just live with your memories as best as you can. Some become neurotics, some would try to drown them out with drinking or drugs. No matter how hard you may try you can't just will them away. But you can make a conscious effort not to wallow in your past miseries. This is what everybody around me, my parents, my friends, the entire community would tell me over and over gain. No wallowing. And it worked.

But some things did stay with me. One is my claustrophobia, undoubtedly the result of so many nights in stifling air raid shelters, in deep darkness, with the ever present fear of possibly getting buried alive. Does anyone now have any idea what it is to be thrown into total darkness, night after night? Almost all of us are now perpetually surrounded by light, even at night, with our streets lit and our night lights in our bedrooms.

When we youngsters were ordered to accompany the night street patrols we were obligated to wear two-inch-size badges made of translucent radioactive materials to make them glow faintly, just enough so see the other person in the total darkness so that we would not bump into each other. We boys were warned never to put these radioactive badges into our pants pockets........ Given the opportunity to be outof the bomb shelters, we would marvel at the night skies lit up by the 'christmas trees', the flares used by the lead bomber plane to locate their targets, followed by the fireworks of explosions, tracer flak and finally the targets in flame - as long as it was at a 'safe' distance. We, of course, thought ourselves indestructible. But then it happened.

On home leave for a few days after the horrors of the Freiburg fire bombing I ignored the air raid alarm, as usual. This time I was not lucky. Some stray bombs came down too close, blowing out windows and taking off parts of our roof. You have never seen anybody racing down three flights of stairs so fast trying to make it into the hated shelter. Something hit the side of my head like a blow of a fist. It did not really hurt but I felt a warm stream flowing down my neck over my sweater and down my pants. In the dim light of the shelter I must have looked awful - there was blood all over me. Mama screamed in anguish imagining the worst. Actually the cut in my scalp was very small but even the smallest head wounds happen to bleed a lot. Once they had overcome their shock they laid down the law - no more playing hero. Get to the shelter!

With my head bandaged much too much for my little scrape, I began to feel like a 'wounded veteran.' Unfortunately there was no time to go around showing off to my friends. Our home no longer livable, we were evacuated to the small farm town of Achdorf, just a few miles from the Swiss border, to live in some tiny rooms above the farm stables. Even the farmers had little food to spare. As fast as they could produce it, it would be confiscated for general distribution, with the army and the Nazis getting most.

To retrieve some food we had left in the basement of our half-destroyed home, about 15 miles away, I was sent back on my sister Anneliese's bicycle with baskets and bags, my own bike too worn and rickety. It had to be done at night because by then the Allied controlled the air space so completely that moving around at daytime you would almost certainly been strafed. The pitch dark narrow country road was total chaos, full of refugees from the advancing Allied armies, with carts pulled by horses, cows and people, all competing for space in the darkness of the winter night, desperately trying to get away, just away. I made it through to our ruined home, scooping up what I could find by groping my way in

the total darkness of our basement, no lights allowed, ever. I also knew to have my ID handy because if suspected to be looting I would be shot on the spot. It was a bitter cold night and somehow I made it back, received with joy, all of us ready to devour what I brought - but to our bitter disappointment most was spoiled, frozen, and the glass jars with preserves broken. Bitter indeed. But it drove home what it meant to deal with hunger.

By then everybody knew that the war was lost and yet the Nazi fanatics forced the continuation of their lost cause with ridiculously insufficient means: no gasoline for the few cars and trucks left, almost no ammunition or medications for the wounded, no food, nothing. The advancing Allied kept pounding the retreating German troops and fleeing civilians who could not move away fast enough, creating havoc, leaving no escape. Switzerland, a much hoped-for refuge was just a couple of miles away but the Swiss had, of course, closed their border. Surrender was dangerous because you would be shot from behind, or hung if caught, mainly by the SS and other incurable Nazis. They were the only ones who had an interest in prolonging the war – before their day of reckoning would come. Can you imagine the horror of seeing a man hung on a tree?

What helped the Nazis to prolong this insane war was the Allied's demand for 'unconditional surrender.' This was cruelly exploited by the Nazi propaganda machine: "Now you see, our enemies are hell bent on destroying Germany, killing all its people, ravaging our women...just see how they bomb our cities." and on and on, giving the Nazis all the justification for forbidding any type of surrender, hanging without trial anyone they suspected of treason. Their reign of terror was unnecessarily prolonged by this fateful decision by the Allied leaders. And, of course, being driven into the corners from where there would be no escape made quite a few German soldiers fight on, even when they wished they could get away somehow.

It was in these chaotic last days of the war when I received the dreaded draft notice, promptly after turning fifteen, to join the 'Volkssturm', the very young and the very old soldiers, the Nazi's last ditch attempt to replenish the depleted ranks of the German fighting forces. Even after just about everything else had broken down, the German drafting offices were still functioning with notorious efficiency. So, in the last senseless few months of the war's insanity I became a member of Germany's fighting forces, pitifully made up of boys and old men, armed with vintage rifles, and in tattering uniforms.

The Volkssturm was meant to stay in our home towns and to defend them once the Allied forces would attack. In the meantime we were to help in rescue efforts after air raids, putting out fires, and patrolling streets during air raids to make sure everybody was in shelters. Overwhelmed, frightened and mostly hungry, we were a sorry lot.

Occasionally, we were guarding Allied POWs until they were taken away to camps. We were under strict orders not to bother them in any form. The plain fact was that we were afraid of them, even though we had the guns and they did not.

Later on I heard that many Allied POWs would complain bitterly of their treatment by their German captors and especially that they had been humiliated by being transported in freight cars (often they would refer to them as 'cattle cars'). Of course, there was no insult intended - that was all that was left of the once famed German rail service. In the last years of the war it was quite normal that all of us would ride in those 'cattle cars.' We were glad to find transportation at all.

In mid-April of 1945, the Allied troupes were about to overrun our home-based defense lines. We were ordered to fall back with the retreating German forces into what we knew would become a total disaster. I was spared the final slaughter. The locals came to my parents saying "you already have lost two of your sons, let's not lose yet another one to this wretched war." With that they hid me and a few other of the town's boys in a narrow gorge (Wutachschlucht), brought some food and blankets, all at the risk of getting hanged if caught by Nazi zealots who were prowling for hapless deserters. It was late April and the nights were still cold.

Sleeping on the rain-soaked ground I never shivered as much in my life. After two days and nights in this dark damp cave-like rock formation, with sporadic gunfighting around us, the townspeople came to tell us that the Allied had taken the town. The next question was how to avoid becoming a POW. We shed our pitiful uniforms, threw away our vintage rifles and slipped away in farmers' clothes, carrying rakes and scythes. Somehow we made it home, whatever and wherever that was.

The war's final convulsions had moved further East, into Bavaria, the German army's last stronghold. In our area the shooting had stopped. We got permission by the occupying French to go back to our Donaueschingen home and fixed it up as best as we could, only to be evicted to make room for a contingent of some 30 Moroccan French colonials who in our area had done much of the fighting for the French. They were primitive, vicious rapists and in their ignorance very destructive. Most of the time there was no water and the toilets were overflowing. So, the Moroccans took the seats out of some of our dining room chairs and put them up in our little garden as their latrines.

Mama was horrified to see them ravage our home, stealing anything we had not squirreled away and breaking so many of the things that our parents had saved through all the previous calamities. It took days of shoveling out filth and debris after they finally had left. They were replaced by French regulars who restored some semblance of order, pretty much stopping the rampant raping and looting. We had seen too many women, even the very young and the very old, running home in tears, sobbing, and more often than not in great pain. Complaining to those in command would not even get you any attention. It took lots of cunning and constant maneuvering to keep Mama safe. Father had managed to move Anneliese into Erlenbad, a nearby convent school, where she was as well protected as possible.

The victors write the history. Therefore, you will not read about these totally unnecessary cruelties - "Our boys would never do this..." Let no one tell you that there is anything good coming from war. Courage is much better shown right here at home, in standing up for your and your fellow citizens' rights, or coming to their rescue when disaster strikes. That may show more heroism than bringing down somebody with your machine gun.

It should be the job of our politicians to keep us out of wars, not to get us into them. But as we would see over and over again, the lure to become a 'president of war,' to be noted as such in the history books, turned out too seductive - even in a democracy like America.

In the End it was All about Survival

The big dangers of the shooting war are real, but so is that daily grind of trying to survive that could wear down even the strongest. And contrary to some romantic notion war does not bring out the best in people.

When food becomes increasingly scarce, trying to get some of it becomes an obsession. Of course, we were given ration cards, but as the war went on, the rations became smaller and smaller. The end of the war did not bring much relief for another two or three years, until the Marshall Plan became effective. In fact, the first year after the war was the worst. We were hungry most of the time, but it was bearable as long as we were confident that the next day we could buy some more food, as little and as lousy as it was. Bread was being stretched by adding bran, until eventually it tasted almost like saw dust. It kept the stomach full and the feeling of hunger down, and may have been good for keeping bowels moving, but its nutritious value was next to nil.

Panic struck when even with ration coupons there simply was no food to buy any more. Often, after standing in line for hours, I had to return home empty-handed, with little hope that the next day would be better. These were the times when Mama's natural skills came to our rescue, making very good use of her Home Economics teachings. She would say that "as long as we have some form of oil or grease we can always cook a wholesome meal". How so, when there was no food to be found at the grocers? She would show us that you can always find some form of food in the meadows and forests - if you only keep your eyes open. No salad to be purchased? Just take dandelion leaves and spice them up with a little sour grass, all growing in abundance in any meadow. Want some soup? Go and pick young nettles and boil them with some mushrooms. Go scavenge for a few potatoes left over in the fields after the harvest. You want some more flavor? Just get some wild onions, abundant in wet meadows.

But for cooking something of substance you needed fat, that was the problem. There just was not any to be had, most of the time. So, we would go to the forests to pick beech nuts from the leaf-covered forest floor, competing with the squirrels. It took many big buckets full of these tiny nuts to yield just a few cups of cooking oil, but what a delicious taste! Of course, that would take many hours of truly back-breaking work, but used judiciously, it would make the best meals from the simplest ingredients.

For us, living in farm country and with so much wild life in the forests surrounding us, there was the occasional deer, rabbit or wild boar, and if you knew the hunters you could always scrounge a bit of the lesser cuts. For Mama, that was enough for her culinary creativity to keep us in reasonably good health. Others did not fare so well, especially the city dwellers who did not have the meadows and forests nearby. Many, many died of hunger in those awful pitiless years.

Our foraging for fresh greens became a regular family outing. Many years later, when just about everything had become available again, Mama still would carry a plastic bag for the herbs she picked on her daily walks through the Gengenbach meadows for her famed herbal teas. There were essentially three varieties: Chamomile, Rose Hip and all purpose tea, a random mixture of any herb that Mama would find along the King river. We would lovingly refer to this unique blend as "Late Harvest Kinzig." There would always be a delightful surprise about its flavors, depending on what herbs happen to be in season.

"Hunger is the best cook". Never waste food. It takes a lot of work to produce it, and there is a finite supply. You also learned that it is not at all necessary to satisfy hunger or thirst instantly. You can safely wait a little. It's good for body and soul.

Whenever we could get the rare permission to travel we would visit our relatives in Rohrbach to get extra food. That was highly illegal because every effort was made by the authorities to distribute all available food evenly to all people, and to prevent black marketing. This was enforced with severe penalties and confiscation, if caught. Like many other women, Mama and Anneliese would stuff little sacks of flour and meat under their dresses to look pregnant, hoping to be safe from intrusive checking by the transit police. Still, the tension!

Nothing bad happened to us on these food smuggling excursions. The policemen had probably already figured out why all of a sudden there were so many 'pregnant' women on the trains...

Those who still had something to barter for food did so. Some greedy farmers would wind up with more luxury item than they had use for, like oriental carpets and jewelry and all kinds of hungry people's family heirlooms. Brother Hermann had bought an accordion for me to encourage my interest in music, but soon it had to be traded for food, pretty much ending my prospects of a musical career.

Next to the constant worries about food came the fight against the cold. The unusually severe winters in the 1940's were sharpened by lack of warm clothing. Whatever clothes we had would be re-made over and over by Mama so that, unlike so many others, we never were in rags. Still, the perpetual shortage of coal for our fancy ceramic stoves ('Kunscht') became hard to take. Fortunately we were surrounded by forests where we were allowed to pick fallen branches to carry home, but nothing bigger than arms-thick pieces. Trudging up and down through the woods was good exercise, perhaps, but again terribly time-consuming, and you could carry only so much on each trip.

But there was always coal at the rail station - locomotives ran on coal. The question was how to get it. Needless to say, that was outright stealing, with severe penalties when caught. Security men with dogs patrolled day and night. We youngsters used the age-old technique of distracting the guards on one end of the coal heap to give us a minute or two to grab a few lumps of coal and then run home with our loot as fast as we could. Lots of time consumed for just keeping a little warm. We survived. Many did not.

Let's be humble about the limits to shape our own futures, but let's not wallow in our misfortunes either. It is not a matter of trying to forget, but rather a matter of learning how to overcome.

Deprivation makes new Rules

Millions had lost their homes and their belongings and had to be given shelter one way or the other. Those fortunate enough to still have a roof over their heads were obligated to take in bombed-out strangers. Then, on top, came the never ending stream of 'displaced persons,' people driven from Eastern German provinces or German speaking minorities in neighboring countries, about ten million of them, all being herded into the devastated West. Everybody had to learn to share the remaining spaces, and in these crowded conditions tempers would often flare. The rub always was to share the kitchen, fighting over scarce food and cooking facilities – remember that there was very little wood, coal or electricity. Should I mention the perpetual annoyance of having to share the only bathroom with a dozen or so strangers, with their often unsavory personal habits?

Rules of moral behavior changed with necessities. During the war it had become an accepted custom to provide a temporary place in your home for soldiers' wives (or girl friends) when they came to visit their men at home base or military hospital. In Donaueschingen we had a rather spacious home right next to the very large army base. Until our place became uninhabitable by repeated bombing we hosted quite a few distant relatives and friends or others who had the proper introduction to enable them to enjoy their men's company before they would be sent back to the horrors of the front to an almost sure death. It was a very charitable thing to do. Mama's only concern (tongue-in-cheek?) was that the beds we provided were being worn out... It taught me early on that a new larger form of morality put charity and generosity before narrow adherence to outdated convention.

Mama, when not busy with our family needs, would often work long hours at the military hospital, a huge complex which toward the end of the war also increasingly housed injured downed Allied airmen. They were kept in a separate section until they had been healed enough to be sent to the POW camps but they were treated just like any other patient with regard to food, medications and medical attention. If there were shortages (and there were many), they were born equally, some later complaints of POWs notwithstanding. Mama often told us about her conversations with the POWs in her very rudimentary English.

The dire needs of the postwar years had created new standards for personal relationships. Many had no roof over their heads, had lost their spouses, and often had no food. So started the proverbial institution of the 'Bratkartoffelverhaeltnis' (literally 'Fried Potato Relationship'), a very practical new form of personal cohabitation where one would supply the roof over your head, the other the food, and both would provide each other the comforts of life, with no particular additional expectations attached to the relationship. Was there anything wrong to befriend lonely war widows? Was satisfying their desperate need for companionship, even their sexual longings, such a bad thing? We did not think so, and most of us who had lived through those trying days will understand. This was not the time and the place to moralize. It was the time and place to be charitable, to help each other.

One of Father's skills as a local leader was the ability to deal effectively with established powerful families, serving as a sort of buffer between them and the war economy. It happened that Donaueschingen, where we were relocated at the outset of the war, is the home base of the Fürstenberg family. I went to the Fürstenberg Gymnasium (German high school) and one of my classmates was Kari von Fürstenberg (he died early after the war in a car accident). With their vast land holdings, the Fürstenberg family supplemented the meat-starved townspeople with often-abundant huntings, and they found in Father the right man to deal with this matter efficiently and without interference by zealots. Whenever my brothers were on leave, they, as many other soldiers of rank, would be invited for a feast at the Fürstenberg castle - we envied them for that. In the end there was something akin to a friendship developing between the families, but after the war this did not survive – I guess they no longer needed us.

Father had successfully implemented a way to ensure survival for us and for all the many people who depended on him. He had a remarkable ability to somehow overcome adversity with whatever limited tools he had available. And he would bring out the best in the people around him especially when despair seemed the only option left. Rather than looking for Germany's stifling bureaucracy he just took action as best he could even when it meant to bend some of the unworkable restrictions of those days. He did not know it then, but in many ways he was living the American ideal of self-reliance.

We, and many, many others, had good reason to admire him for all he had done to help them survive. Once again he had been the leader that his times needed, just as he had lead them through the German depression and the Nazi terror.

The War ended, but not our Troubles

Growing up in times of great upheavals, deprivation and deep social changes has its benefits which, of course, are not at all visible while trudging through the misery. But a lot of learning was happening. I sometimes wonder how people go through life without ever having experienced much of its ups and downs. How can they see the whole complexity, fragility and the meaning of their lives?

No matter what was one's political orientation, losing the war was a terrible blow to every German's mind, seeing Germany so utterly destroyed and disgraced for all the horrors that it had inflicted on so many. We had known all along that the day of reckoning would be coming and that we Germans would pay a huge price for all the horrors that Germany had bestowed of the world. It could be no surprise to the Germans that their victors would extract more than their 'pound of flesh' from Germany and us Germans. The Allied conquerors had come to Europe as liberators, but that would not apply to Germany - they made it plenty clear that they were here to rule with an iron hand.

Life under Allied occupation was a bitter and traumatic experience, even after the original widespread rapes and looting had stopped. Whatever factories were still operating would be dismantled for 'Reparations' to compensate all the countries conquered by Germany during the war for the destructions and their suffering. Just as Germany's cities and its infrastructure were totally destroyed, so was the Germans' spirit. It took true patriotism to get the country out of its state of desperation. Father was one of those fearless leaders who were ready to squarely face up to the necessity to deal with Germany's dire circumstances.

There was strict military rule, with early evening curfew. I spent several nights in the local military jail because sometimes we would be late coming back from school, and sometimes we simply dallied a bit to bait the military police. You could not leave town without a specific permit. The allied occupation forces were much afraid that there would be some form of continued resistance by some die-hard Nazis after the war was officially over, but with very rare exception, no such insurgency happened. The Germans truly had enough, and also because Germans were brought up to accept the big decisions imposed upon them. Nevertheless, there was much fear on all sides. In some places, revenge killings took place. But at least we could now rely again on a well functioning legal system, free from the demoralizing fears of the Nazi terror.

The Gengenbach townspeople had called Father back to become their Mayor again. Times were terrible. His first concern was to protect his people from the ravages of undisciplined occupation troops. Also, un-repenting Nazis were still there, sowing discord and occasionally throwing some ugly accusations at him. He wanted to rally his people, to help them make some sense of the calamities of war, defeat and daily misery. His thoughtful and uplifting "Proclamation to the People of Gengenbach" became famous and would be emulated by many other community leaders in the area:

An sämtliche Einwohner der Stadt Gengenbach!

In einer ungewöhnlich schweren Zeit trete ich mein Amt wieder an. Nach einem Zusammenbruch ohne Gleichen sehen wir vor uns ein Trümmerfeld, wie es die Menschheit in seiner ganzen Trostlosigkeit bisher nicht gekannt hat. Trümmer in den Arbeitsstätten und Wohnungen, Trümmer im Verkehr, Handel und Gewerbe, Trümmer in den Familien, in den Herzen und Seelen der deutschen Menschen. Unendliches Leid und Weh ist damit über das deutsche Volk gekommen.

Heute müssen wir uns klar und eindeutig vor Augen halten, daß wir den Krieg verloren und die sich daraus ergebenden Folgen zu tragen haben. So sehen wir uns einer Sachlage gegenüber, die ohne alle Illusionen betrachtet werden muß. Was ist zu tun?

Vor allem ist absolute Ruhe und Ordnung notwendig. Den für uns maßgebenden Anordnungen der Militärregierung ist williger und unbedingter Gehorsam zu leisten. Klarheit und Offenheit, Anstand und Würde haben unsere Haltung zu bestimmen. In unserem Wiederaufbau steht uns ein langer und steiniger Weg bevor und trotzdem müssen wir ihn mit Mut und Vertrauen beschreiten. Viel Geduld wird notwendig sein. Die gemeinsame Not muß in nachhaltiger gemeinsamer Leistung gemildert und schließlich überwunden werden. Jeder einzelne muß sich aber bewußt werden, daß nur eine ungestörte Gemeinschaft der Tat uns helfen kann. Alles muß unterlassen werden, was dem Einzelnen und der Gemeinschaft Schaden bringt. Der wirtschaftliche Aufbau hat zur Voraussetzung eine geistige und seelische Erneuerung und Gesundung unseres Volkes, vorab unserer Jugend. Sie muß sich gründlich abwenden von der einseitig betonten und gesibten körperlichen Ertüchtigung. Eine tiefe religiöse Gläubigkeit und das Bewußtsein der Verantwortlichkeit vor Gott muß wieder Gemeingut des Volkes werden. Nur so werden wir einer Verwilderung der Sitten und der Moral vorbeugen, nur so können wir unserem Volke wieder im Laufe der Zeit einen ehrenvollen Platz in der Gemeinschaft der Völker erringen.

Unserer engen Heimat aber gilt unsere besondere Liebe und Hoffnung. Mögen alle das Gebot der Stunde erkennen und tatkräftig mithelfen, die unserer Stadt geschlagenen schweren Wunden zu heilen.

Um diese Mitarbeit bitte ich

Mack, Bürgermeister.

Gengenbach, den 22. Juni 1945.

To all People of the Town of Gengenbach:

In a time of unparalleled upheaval I am resuming my office as your Mayor. After a cataclysmic war we are facing a vast field of destruction that humanity has never seen before, destruction of our work place, our homes, and desolation of our families and the heart and soul of us Germans. Unimaginable suffering and despair has been visited upon us, and by us. We must face clearly and without any embellishment of the facts that we have lost the war and must accept responsibility for all its consequences. We have to do this without illusions. What are we to do?

First and above all, we must keep calm, and keep order. We have no choice but to follow the directives of the (Allied) Military Government without resistance and reservation. However, we should do this with clarity of mind, openness, decency and dignity. Before us is a long and rocky road to rebuild our town and country, and in spite of all thorny issues we must proceed with courage, patience and in the confidence in our basic values. We all must share in the common struggle to overcome deprivation that is hurting all of us, by sustained unselfish cooperation. Each one of us must realize that only working together can help us. We must stay clear of disturbances and of any action that would hurt any one of us or our community.

Reconstruction of our homes and towns must be accompanied by a profound spiritual renewal and healing of all our people, above all of our young ones. They in particular have to turn away from their previous teachings and from one-sided emphasis of the physical. A deep religious responsibility before God and to our neighbors will help to bind our people together again. Only by returning to our traditional customs and morality can we hope to regain, over time, an honorable place in the Community of Nations.

We have a special love and hope for our home town. Let all of us recognize what is needed to heal the spiritual and bodily wounds of our communities. Let us do the hard work together. For this, I am asking for your cooperation.

- Gengenbach, June 22, 1945, Mack, Mayor

Our old residence, the Rathaus, was half destroyed. We were given a floor above the kindergarten school building, large by

standards of the rest. We too had to share our space – in our situation not with refugee families, but with officers of the French occupation forces, and later with young French teachers who were sent by forward-looking French administrators to teach in our schools, one of the many efforts to help overcome the Germans' the French' hatred and distrust of each other.

I think Father did not quite realize at first how difficult his job would be under the harsh military occupation by the French. He was trying hard to get the best possible deals for the people of Gengenbach, by defusing some of the more onerous demands by the French. On the other hand he had to make everybody understand that not complying with the dictates of the military government would lead to even harsher measures. Predictable, he would be criticized by all sides: The French would berate him when he protested their vengeful taking the best homes, throwing the owners out in the street and confiscating their valuables, or when he was dragging his feet on their much hated demands for dismantling of what was left of our factories. Predictably and unfairly some Germans would say that he did not do enough to help them against the French, not wanting to understand that in truth he had done much more than any one else to fight their edicts. To his chagrin he found himself caught too often in the middle, and we as a family felt the resentment from both the French and our own people. It was a delicate balancing act, and a thankless task.

Well remembered are the great postwar European leaders who tried to put order back into the lives of the nations that had been hell bent on destroying each other for so long. They were remembered in history as the right leaders at the right time - Adenauer in Germany, Monet and Schuman in France, and, of course, Marshall in America. But we should not forget the thousands of local leaders that shouldered the often thankless task of picking up the pieces left by the Nazi war, who worked so hard to get people and neighbors back together, to learn again how to live in peace with each other. They were the real patriots. Father was one of them.

Governing, just like management, is a complicated job, whether big or small. You cannot do right for everyone all the time. In the short term, cunning may help, but principled pursuit of what's possible is more durable. And before passing judgement, as the saying goes, always try to put yourself in the other guy's shoes.

Father would negotiate hard with the French for concessions to ease their often harsh occupation policies. One was to allow some Gengenbachers to get hunting rifles even when firearms were still forbidden for Germans, so that we could supplement food supply from the over-abundance of wild boar. The occupying French were avid hunters of all other game but they usually shunned the often dangerous wild boar. Thus the boar had become too numerous, doing a lot of damage to critical harvests. On these hunts we youngsters were the 'drivers,' hoping our hunters knew what they were doing, but the prospects of bringing home a good cut of fresh meat always made up for the risks.

For me, there was a melodramatic twist in these wild boar hunts. One of the keepers of the rifles was a good friend of our family. His beautiful wife had taken quite a liking to me, and I learned a lot from her about relations between men and women, more than what my parents were able or willing to teach me. It was all within the framework of her own well developed, down-to-earth morality and her unquestioned dedication to her husband. Somehow I assumed that her husband must have viewed our relationship askance, and I feared the wrath of a suspicious husband coming down on me. As we would be out there hunting – I as a 'driver' in the bushes, in front of the line of hunters, and he, the hunter, with a loaded gun – my imagination went wild, fearing that one day….but of course no such thing ever happened, and he most likely found my relationship with his wife quite okay.

Reconstruction started. Every able-bodied surviver was recruited to help rebuilding the many homes damaged to varying degrees by bombs, artillery and incendiaries. First priority was given to repairing roofs, to stop water damage. Roofing in most parts of Europe consists of the traditional picturesque reddish-brown ceramic tiles that give the towns such cheerful roof lines. They were, of course, mostly not available. My friend Hans Weber's dad was an architect and he came up with the idea for us to make roofing tiles from mortar reinforced with chopped straw - there was plenty of cement left over from abandoned bunker projects, and sand was abundant down on the shores of the Kinzig river.

Hans and I got to work. We built wooden molds, pressed our mortar mix into them and left them over night to cure. It was a laborious process, but the towns people would buy them from us as fast as we could make them. Top production: according to my diary 1,700 tiles with a four 'men' team in a twelve hour day! It was my first foray into a manufacturing business. Soon these drab grey tiles could be seen all over town mixed in with the much prettier red ceramics - it made for rather funny roof patterns. Trouble was that our tiles did not last through the severe winter frost cycles. We had visions of much repeat business next season but it was not to be. Ceramic tiles had become available again and our cement tile manufacturing scheme faltered and so did my hopes for becoming 'Mr.Concrete Tiles.' But some Gengenbach old-timers still remember how we saved their homes from potentially disastrous water damage, at least over the winter snows and rains!

Every structure that could be used as temporary housing for refugees was requisitioned and made into living quarters, albeit very simplistic ones - better than not having a roof over your head at all. Father had suggested I help one particular war widow from some Eastern country to convert an old gardens shed for her use. Working side by side it did not take long for us to get very close, and we started doing a lot of things together that were totally unrelated to the job. Were my parents wondering why it would take me so long to finish the work? Did they know what we were doing? Following the peculiar codes of silence of those times there was nothing said one way or the other.

Father had the foresight to bring to Gengenbach a very well known language school (Vorbeckschule) that had been bombed out of Mannheim. Bringing that school to Gengenbach was obviously difficult (just imagine the uproar against having to absorb even more outsiders!) but it was also the most significant effort to give Gengenbach a new face: no longer just a sleepy old town, but now with a new cultural face. The school's owner, Frau Charlotte Vorbeck, quite the aristocratic figure, was initially a difficult customer, but became a close personal friend, adding quite a bit of her worldliness to our family's ways. Several other academic institutions were to follow, making Gengenbach into a college town, its magnificent Baroque abbey now an IT College.

We also learned a lot from our French boarders, not only linguistically. I remember fondly the Lapalus, a mother and daughter from Dijon, Mlle. Bideau from Chaumont, and Andre Laxague from Tarbes. They were very fine people and became real friends, understanding well the huge problems we all were facing to overcome hatred and fear between Germans and our French neighbors. With all these connections, and because Father wanted it so, we spent many weeks visiting nearby France, to hone our French and to give us a better understanding of the French views of us Germans, in times when animosity on both sides was still running high. Our visits to brother Waldemar's grave site in the immense

Niederbronn war cemetery near Strasbourg were always emotional but served to teach us the futility of wars. In the end, when everybody is exhausted from all the fighting you will always have to go back to live together again with your neighbors.

There is no end to the possibilities of life's surprises. Some fifty years after the war, living in St. Barths in the French Caribbean, we had befriended a French lady, Monique LeVeque. Hearing my first name, she asked about my origin – German, yes, but from where, and after a few iterations, Gengenbach. Well, as a teenager she had lived in the neighboring town of Offenburg at the time when I went to Gymnasium there. Her father, an officer in the French army, was stationed there, in charge of the relations with the post-war local German community leaders. It is quite certain that he and my father had dealings with each other in a most difficult time for both the French and the Germans. So, here in the French Caribbean we find a new friend with an old family connection of some sort. Is there a better way to show the absurdity of troubles between nations?

What was it really like for our family to live in the aftermath of the war ? What had to be done to get out from under its horrors, its deprivations? Somehow, life had to go on.

I had developed an interest in technical matters. Hands-on work in reconstruction and maintaining farm machinery had given me some level of practical skills. One of my early interests was to build (very) simple radio sets. Most radios had been confiscated by the Nazis, and those that had survived the war were often 'requisitioned' by the occupation forces. But there were discarded German army radios left here and there, valuable sources of parts, especially the essential vacuum tubes. My radios were simplistic sets, 'Rube-Goldberg' style, fixed to receive only the local station, but in those days that was better than nothing. You learned to do with whatever parts you found and forget about the looks. People didn't care for appearance, they just wanted to hear the broadcast. The few radios I built I traded for extra food in Rohrbach (some old-timers there are still talking about that). For this and other tinkering, my parents gave me a small corner space in the attic. The roof was leaking, most of the few attic window were broken and boarded up, but the few that were still intact gave me a splendid view of the old city towers and the park below the city walls. I did a lot of day-dreaming there also.

And then, out of the blue, I fell madly in love. Mama's distant cousin showed up soon after the war with her daughter, Irmgard, a

few years older than I, and her older sister. They had lost everything, their home, their belongings, husband and father. Somehow they found their way to us, hungry, exhausted from days of travel on overcrowded trains, with nothing but the clothes on their backs. To make room for them, I was moved to my attic corner. Mama worked her magic to nurse them back to life with the little we had to give.

And Irmgard and I fell in love, with all the wonderful and immature emotions of teenagers and the furtive meetings in my attic room. It threatened to get totally out of control until Father stepped in with sage and stern advice: "Too young, not ready for responsibility, unable to control yourself, and before you know it, your ardent puppy love will fizzle out, so, snap out of it!" It took me while to find out how right he was. Sure, young infatuation is overwhelming and can make you lose your mind for a while, but rarely does it mature into real lasting love.

Irmgard moved away after a few weeks of turmoil and passion, and we soon lost track of each other. The picture of her family speaks volumes: from the comfort of their middle class life they were reduced to base deprivation. In their previous life, they would have been too proud to show themselves in this state of poverty. *War*.

Worn out by wars, the loss of two sons, his bitter life under the Nazis, and his thankless efforts to help pick up the pieces after Germany's defeat, Father gave up his work at 70, and died at 76, after a brief bout with stomach cancer. His funeral was attended by hundreds of his friends and relatives who came to pay their respects to a role model of patriotic civic service, father and husband. In

gratitude of all he had done for his beloved Gengenbach, his grave in the beautiful Gengenbach cemetery will be kept forever in the

care of the town. It is marked by an impressive and artistically remarkable granite block designed by Anneliese' architect husband Johannes. The family grave would become Mama's resting place fifteen years later. It also carries the inscriptions of my brothers names who had to die so far away from their home.

To Father's great regret, he never was given the pleasure of seeing his grandchildren. Mama did better. She died peacefully at 96, having enjoyed her six grandchildren, Anneliese's Cajatan and Claude from Luzern, and our four sons, with many great family visits and her lengthy stays with us in America, a loving mother-in-law to ever so patient Francesca who loved her right back.

Mama and Father will forever live on in our memories.

<O>

Phases of our Lives

THE STUDENT

"When you know better you do better."

- Maya Angelou

Phases of our Lives

Schooling for Success

During the last six months of the war, and the six months after, we had no school. Most teachers were in the army, some doing rescue work and most of them occupied with their own survival. There was little food, no heat, and the school buildings that were not destroyed were used by the military, often for make-shift hospitals. Schools finally opened again in early winter of 1946. You have never seen a group of youngsters as eager to get back into the class room. After years of going hungry and spending our wake hours clearing the rubble from our destroyed cities, getting back to learning was just fine. Hard to explain to today's youngsters!

I was now starting the second half of Gymnasium in the nighboring city of Offenburg. (European 'Gymnasium' is generally seen as the equivalent of American 'High School' plus two years of College}. Remember that at that time only one out of ten elementary student would make it into the Gymnasium level 'high school', a fundamental difference to the American system. Studying was very serious stuff for us. We had lost an entire year of schooling and had to work hard to make up. We knew that the only way to save us from the misery of unemployment or the menial work of reconstruction was to succeed at school. Access to University was limited to two or three percent of the population only, with preference given to veterans and returning POWs. You can easily see the competitive pressures.

Just to get to and from school was a big problem. The Offenburg Schiller Gymnasium was seven miles from Gengenbach, a bit more than walking there on a daily basis. First, we went by the only truck left in Gengenbach, owned by Herr Walker. It was powered by a wood gasifier, then a quite common and in the end a useful way to substitute the nearly non-existent petroleum fuels (living in the Black Forest had its advantages). In winter we would fight for a place near the hot gasifier tank to keep warm. On the open truck bed there were  wooden benches on its sides, enough seating for only about one quarter of us. The rest would be standing, swaying as the truck would be lumbering over the ruts in the roadway.

A year later the railways started again. In movies you can sometimes see how these trains were hopelessly overcrowded: we thought nothing of riding in between cars or hanging on to the outside, but riding on the roof was not allowed. Freight cars were just fine. Well, that was all that was left of the once so proud

German railways. We were grateful to have transportation at all. Once we could get parts to refurbish our old bicycles we became more independent.

To catch up our workload was huge, but our will to learn was just as big. Everybody wanted to lay a foundation to get us out of the misery of the war years and the tough times after. Our work load was unrelenting, by necessity so much greater than in today's schools. Gymnasium took nine years (age 10 to 19), University a minimum of four years. Gymnasium gave you a very broad education in just about every cultural and science fields, the concept of 'Allgemeinbildung,' which loosely translates to English as the type of 'overarching knowledge of the world' that would be close to the concept of a 'liberal arts college' but with lots of math and sciences in addition to literature in German, French, English and Latin, music and history, lots of history, first the Nazi version, then the much more balanced one written in post-war Germany. We certainly saw that history is always written by the victors.

It came as a surprise to many Americans that even during the war years there was great emphasis on English studies. The 'party-line' explanation was that after Germany would have conquered the British Empire, it would be important for us to be able to conduct their affairs in their language. Knowing a lot better, our teachers would accompany these periodic propaganda pieces with a "wink-wink," telling us in effect that we better do well in English classes because it would come in handy for survival once the Allied would occupy Germany. I had nine years of intensive English, and it would indeed serve me well. Even today, European schooling is more intensive in basics, but American schooling excels in developing independent thinking and social skills.

My classmates had very different talents, some quick-witted, some methodical, some excelling in math and science, some in languages. There was very little organized physical education, civics and social studies which are so much more a part of US schooling. Ours was all academics, intensive, with English at age ten, Latin and French at fourteen. Language studies were aiming at the ability not only to read and write, but to translate even complex texts back and forth. For example, in English we read Dickens' "A Christmas Carol" and Shakespeare plays, some in modern English, some in

German, with much memorizing of key passages. There was much singing, 'music appreciation' and even theatre. My first forage into acting was during the last months of the war as the lead in Schiller's hilarious comedy "The Nephew posing as his Uncle." It was cut short after a roaringly successful opening night when our school was hurriedly converted to a military hospital the next days.

The ones who succeeded in this demanding school environment did so mainly because their families would make sure that they did their homework, at least three hours, six days a week. We had small classes – 26 at the most, and developed close friendships. We still have class reunions every so often at different places wherever the surviving class mates now live.

The Offenburg Schillergymnasium was for boys only. Girls attended a separate school, just because of tradition. As an exception, we had one girl, Gudrun Gramlich, whose father had been school principal earlier and had given in to his daughter's determination to be with the boys. She was like a sister to us, and quite competitive, keeping up with all our doings. We had little school sports, but made up for it with much serious hiking and camping in the many Black Forest mountain huts, built for that purpose. Mostly in co-ed groups we learned about personal relations on that level; we were just buddies. The American concept of 'dating' or 'going steady' was not known to us and actually would have been frowned upon, not on moral grounds but because it would rob young people from the opportunity to get to know others.

I could see that intelligence is usually not spread evenly over all aspects of the functioning of the human brain. Most of us are 'intelligent' in some areas, like math or languages or social skills, and often less so in others. Just look at a genius like Einstein or Edison: they were total failures socially. Or Hitler, the scourge of Germany, Europe and much of the rest of the world. There is no denying that he was excellent as orator, but mediocre as artist, and an absolute moron in strategy: how could anybody with any level of 'intelligence' start a multi-front war and on top ensure the wrath of the world by his inhumanity?

The pressures to succeed were great indeed, but there was also plenty of fun and games. Given the rigidly enforced discipline, it did not take much to get into trouble. I was very much a part of it, but my friend Karl Schuelj was the acknowledged master of irreverent fun and mischief. At one time, reading Goethe's "Faust," we picked the one raunchy scene, "Auerbach's Dungeon," as our theme for a secret beer party in the school's basement, of all places ("We are as happy as a bunch of drunken pigs..."- actual quote!). School master Spreter took us to task and used the most awful threat of expulsion that would have ended our hopes for a decent career. Needless to say, his threat was an empty one, in the end undermining his and the school's authority. Father only laughed at the pompous notice of our misdeeds.

By far our most stupid prank was staging a protest against some new study plans perceived as onerous. We assembled at the ornate wrought iron school gate with a sign "KZ" (Concentration Camp). That hit a raw nerve, given the great sensitivity (1947) about the

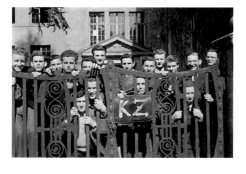

horrendous Nazi concentration camps. It was a sick joke. We were told never, ever again to do anything that would even remotely poke fun at this awful part of German history. Some things are indeed so serious that they cannot be excused.

We did plenty of other stupid things, just as you would expect from a bunch of restless teenagers. The Rhine became our swimming hole, very clean at the time and in easy bicycle distance. The Rhine, of course, is also the border with France, then heavily guarded on both sides. Anyway, we would swim across this mighty river, and as we would approach the French side, we would speak to each other in our

Alsatian-style French, loud enough, so that the border patrols would think we were one of them, 'returning' to shore. When it got to close for comfort, we would jump back into the river to swim back home, repeating the same language

gig the other way around. On the way across we would sometimes swim onto one of the great river barges moving slowly upstream, low in the water with coal for Switzerland, trying to hitch a ride up-river, back to our starting point. Looking back I can only shake my head at this folly.

Winter in the Black Forest brought lots of snow in the mountains for skiing with very primitive equipment and with little regard for safety. We would build our own ski jumps higher and higher, up to a point where none of us could land standing up, a potentially lethal game. When our parents found out, they would give us their sternest talking-to, to little avail ("don't do it again, boys!"). There were very few ski  lifts which we never used, partly because we had no money, and partly we thought of them to be there only for sissies. Well, it was splendid exercise. We were in great shape. There were good friendships, but my best friends were 'Karle' Schuelj and Guenter Petermann, who much later would also find his way to America.

Like in most European countries, graduating from Gymnasium (the German Abitur) is a really big deal. It is based on a grueling

two week long exam covering the entire eight or nine years of Gymnasium curriculum. Success or failure would determine your future for the rest of your life. Everything would depend on it. The seriousness of this milestone is such that many would have nightmares about it for years to come, especially those who had had failed.

Right or wrong, successful completion of the Gymnasium years places you among the 'educated' of your community.

But the even more important next step is deciding on the right future profession, and then getting enrolled at university. In my days, only one out of five Abitur graduates could hope to gain access to this final elevation into the 'professional elite'.

There was no doubt in my mind that this is what I wanted to do. And no surprise: my parents were solidly behind me. Actually, they expected nothing less from me. There was also the tacit understanding that I would somehow make up for my two brothers' lost opportunity to have been chosen for the same academic career.

It was almost that it was now up to me to show the world that our family had emerged strong from the Nazi terror, from war and the devastating loss of my two brothers, and from the loss of the family fortune in the German hyper-inflation. Yes, we were still there, and we shall be the respected family again, and I wanted to be one of those that would count!

An Engineer in the Making

Competition for a place at university was brutal. Gymnasium grades way above average were needed - this I had. However, preference was given to war veterans and especially to returning POWs, many having suffered terribly in Russian labor camps. I did get admitted to the prestigious Karlsruhe Engineering School, just about guaranteeing a good place in the feverish German reconstruction economy. Industry was the place to be.

The Karlsruhe Engineering School (later to become a full-fledged University) was the oldest and the most demanding one in Germany. Quite a few world-class engineering feats had come from there in its long history. The one which would become very much a part of my professional life was Prof. Fritz Haber's nitrogen fixation process. Haber had found a way to take nitrogen from air and by combining it with hydrogen to convert it into ammonia, and from there into agricultural fertilizer. Long after Haber had passed away I had the obligatory stint in his laboratory which to this day is being maintained meticulously as a unique example of an invention that saved untold millions from starvation.

I know that this does not resonate much with most people and even those who may have heard about it in their chemistry classes probably never quite appreciated how this seemingly mundane invention had changed the world. Am I exaggerating? Just think about it - without this relatively cheap fertilizer there would be no way to feed the now almost seven billion people on this earth, up from just one billion some 100 years ago. Yeah, I know - as you read this the 'Greens' are telling you that 'synthetic fertilizers' make bad food and that we could feed ourselves just as well 'organically.' Well, it just is not so. If our food now is so bad how come we live longer and healthier lives now? And as to 'organic' food - have you forgotten the Irish famine, the perpetual hunger of the Italians before they left for America? They did not think that highly of the meager yields of their 'organically' fertilized soils.

Haber's commercial success was largely the result of his close cooperation with Germany's budding chemical industry which had the capability to translate his laboratory discoveries into huge production facilities within just a few years in the early 1900s. It would become the pattern in Germany for the close ties between its engineering schools and its industry. It would almost guaranty a prosperous career for those who were willing to undergo the rigorous training in these industry-dominated schools. Would I ever have thought that just two years after graduation I would get a job in a brand new chemical plant - producing fertilizer with Haber's process? Well, you just never know...

Needless to say I was very proud getting into engineering school. I knew very well that a lot of hard work would be ahead of me and I was ready and willing, or so I thought.

But first there were two more hurdles before my engineering studies could begin: I had to spend six months in the reconstruction work of the bomb-damaged school buildings, and then, as a prerequisite for engineering studies, one year as apprentice in different industries, six months up front, and the rest between semesters. My reconstruction assignment: picking bricks from rubble and cleaning them for re-use. I resented these six months, not so much because of the hard work, but we aspiring students thought that we should not be forced to delay our studies while millions of unemployed would have liked very much to have our reconstruction jobs at that time. There were two reasons given for this policy: first, there was no money to pay hired workers, and, equally important, it would make us appreciate much more the privilege of being permitted to study.

The apprenticeship periods were meant to be hard - first because of the often grimy and unsafe work places, because of the long hours (ten hour days quite the norm then, Saturdays also), and also because the industrial workers often made life difficult for us. There was still a lot of class tension. Thus, we often wound up with the most disagreeable jobs, but there was valuable teaching here also. Example: it happens that my hands are very sensitive to heat. During my tour of duty in a foundry, it didn't take them long to find out about my heat sensitivity, and they systematically assigned me to the hottest jobs – no gloves then.

There is great wisdom in making engineering student do this practical work. Not only do you learn first hand how things are manufactured, but you also got to understand something about the mindset of a factory worker.

These real life lessons were of huge significance. A stint in the coal mines was required to see first hand what working in a mine really meant, in the oppressively narrow and dark shafts. Learning to actually do manufacturing work also was of great help in our engineering studies, creating a much deeper understanding of the basics of engineering, as opposed to the largely theoretical courses in many modern engineering schools.

German universities and engineering schools were owned and controlled by the Ministry of Education who set uniform curriculum and exam standards for all schools. As a result, earning a Diploma would automatically give you a license to practice your profession. The American concept of needing to pass a separate 'Professional License' exam (for each State of the Union!) before being able to practice any profession, engineering or law or medicine is rooted in the fact that the curriculum and the teaching standards in most higher learning institutions here are not set and controlled by a central education authority.

By all standards, the quality of teaching and the depth of learning in our schools were very good indeed. The enormous pressures to succeed, together with the solid foundations from Gymnasium, made for very good studying habits, absolutely necessary to deal with great work loads by unbending concentration and sheer hard work. Nothing less would do.

It also showed me that the dismal state of the physical plant, the half-ruined school buildings, the primitive facilities, and no heating, no student centers and none of the trappings of modern schooling, had little effect on the quality of learning. It was our determination to succeed and our teachers' skills and demands that made the difference. I had many opportunities later in my life to double-check the validity of these observations in my experience in US engineering schools where I would do quite a bit of lecturing and served on their Boards.

Today we think we can improve schooling with more money for ever better buildings, facilities and popular sports programs: it is a monumental waste of money, as none of this really matters. Teachers do, and students' determination.

Altogether life as a student in the period from 1949 to 1954 was not easy. Most of the school's facilities were still in ruins, our student quarters primitive, food scarce and social life practically non-existent. I started out staying in a Catholic student home. It was crowded and noisy, with depressing rooms. It was impossible to do serious studying there. Then we discovered that this place (as several other of this type) was actually run by a group of strangely radical leftist Jesuits. There were these endless discussions among students whether and how these Jesuit politics would fit into our real life experience. I was one of the youngest residents there; most were war veterans and had lived a lot already and were not about to submit to yet another form of coercion.

In any event, I felt a need for more independence and when things got a little better I found a two bedroom attic to share with a Norwegian student, Olaf Soerum, in the quite stately home of a leading local jeweler, the Staub family. In the three years there they gave us a lot more than our rooms, integrating us into their family.

I paid them partly by tutoring their two rambunctious teenage sons. For food, we had to fend for ourselves. Pooling my steady supply of butter and onions from Rohrbach, and Olaf's brown goat cheese and canned herring from his parents in Oslo kept us from being hungry and allowed us to concentrate on our studies, rather than having to hunt for food all the time.

I got also a lot of help from the family of an adopted son of my grandparents on Mama's side. As a part of the social safety net system in the late 1800s, many reasonably well-to-do families would 'adopt' (not legally, but socially) orphans, and my grandparents did that with Emil Thomae, who then married a distant relative of ours, settled in Karlsruhe and became quite successful in the furniture business. He was basically a nice man, but quite cantankerous and always feeling a bit the underdog. In spite of all the love and care he had received from my grandparents, he had never overcome the fact of having been an orphan. His daughter Ursula was pretty and very nice but too young for me. They generously included me in many wonderful family affairs, dinners and outings, enjoying excursions in their black Mercedes, a treat at that time. Eventually Herr Thomae would even include me in his weekly "Stammtisch," rubbing shoulders with Karlsruhe notables.

It turned out that my cousin Paul, with whom I had spent so much time in earlier years in Rohrbach, had his student pad in the very same street as I. Since he was two years older than I he had seen much more of the war than I. He had lost his right arm in a battle quite near his home town, in the last hours of the war, and even with one arm he was studying architecture requiring a lot of drawing work. To my great regret we did not spend much time together in Karlsruhe. As a wounded veteran he had been admitted to study much before me, and thus was in effect three years ahead of me, so that we overlapped one year only. Even though, in hindsight, it was a big mistake on my side because we could have had such a good time together and could have given much support to each other.

Social life during my student times was not what one would like to think. First of all, at Engineering School our workload was immense, compared with most other university courses. We had little money, little time and also no private quarters. Against the backdrop of a country still in recovery, there was tremendous pressure to finish in the shortest time possible, with good marks, to get a job quickly. There were few women then at engineering school, but fortunately through my parents' connections I met a few young women my age. My relations with them were limited: in addition to the lack of time and money, I had been brought up with quite strict rules of social behavior. Not that my parents had any problems with sex and love making: they were quite matter-of-fact and certainly no hypocrites, but all the same they had made a very strong point in demanding honesty, consideration and social graces. Above all they told me never to make false promises, like declarations of "never ending love" when my objectives were of a much more immediate nature. Perhaps my parents' demands did not help my love life very much at that time, but I found out later that for my own self-respect and for a solid foundation of my future family life their teachings were right on.

Unlike college here we developed few lasting friendships. Remember: times were very difficult. Everybody was pretty much out for themselves. Our priorities were to survive and to finish school as fast as possible. Few students chose to belong to the traditional fraternities, and very few indeed joined the saber fighting kind, a hotbed of ultra-conservatives and un-repenting right-wingers, outlawed but still hanging on, but pretty well forgotten by now. Guided by my parents' progressive outlook I wanted to remain independent, free of the constraints of life in an organization. I did join the fencing group and the riding club and became quite good at both sports. From my Rohrbach farming days I was comfortable with horses and pretty well knew what made them go. I became quite competitive in jumping, less interested in dressage. Later on, in Baton Rouge and then in New Jersey, I would own horses but I gave up riding when work and traveling took over.

My student years taught me what it takes to be an engineer. It is not just learning all about physics and chemistry and mathematics -

you also learned how to deal with a seemingly unsurmountable work load. You learned that there is no place for procrastination and for simple cop-outs. It does prepare you well for the realities of the workplace. After the ordeals of engineering school my future life in the money making world did not seem so threatening any more.

But as so often, life would have different things in store for me.

Onward to America!

As graduation from the Karlsruhe Engineering School (without any ceremony then) was getting closer, the Chair of the Chemical Engineering department, Prof. Kirschbaum suggested that I enter the university teaching career, under his tutorship. Becoming a teacher in the German university system was a very coveted career, with automatic life tenure. My parents thought of it as the pinnacle in our family's achievements, in their minds putting us squarely into the ranks of Germany's elite. It would be hard for me not to accept.

The time-honored first step was to be appointed 'Hilfsassistent', literally 'helper to the assistant.' It was not very glamourous - mainly supervising work in the laboratories and keeping students from doing foolish things. But is also gave me the 'inside track' for my master's thesis ("Simultaneous Heat and Mass Transfer") in the school's very large industry-supported pilot plants.

There was lots of excitement in this seemingly boring task. Together with a gaggle of undergraduates I was working with mixtures of water and alcohol to study the azeotrope (the strange physics problem when trying to distill alcohol to near 100% concentration). Many evenings, after a long day of breathing alcohol-laden air we would literally be drunk, but curiously without the hangover.

In any case the prospect of entering the august ranks of university professors was intriguing. My father was elated but I had mixed feelings. I was rather dreaming of a career in industry, the place to be at that time. In those days of Germany's feverish reconstruction programs, industrial firms would line up at our engineering school to snatch up every reasonably promising new graduate.

But I also wanted to see more of the world. One way would be to sign up for overseas duty with an international engineering firm, and I actually interviewed with one of them, the Hamburg based Toepfer Group. But the areas where they would send us young engineers were mostly places where you would not really wanted to be, like building refineries in Saudi Arabia. I was not sure where to turn.

Prof. Kirschbaum made that decision for me, in a roundabout way - he suggested that I should fill out an application that he had on his desk for a one year post-graduate scholarship in the US ("....after all, you have done quite a few translations for me of English and American engineering papers, and therefore you, not me, should be the one to apply..."). At that time very few Germans were allowed or could afford traveling outside Germany, not even to neighboring countries. Certainly going to America and to stay there for a year would be a big deal indeed. Dutifully, with no great expectation of success, I filled out the many forms and sent them in. And, low and behold, a few months later I found a letter in my mail from America with a one year Fulbright scholarship – everything included.

I was elated. Of course, I did not know a thing about this scholarship and I had no idea where in America I would be sent. But who wants to ask questions! (Whenever I say 'America' in this book I mean, of course, the United States of America).

Named after its initiator, Senator William Fulbright, his program was one of the rare examples of truly great statesmanship and a cosmopolitan spirit that normally would not have been expected from politicians, especially from one coming from Arkansas. Already as an Oxford Rhodes Scholar he had acquired a good understanding of the world outside his native Middle-America. Later in his eminent Congressional career he would courageously oppose McCarthy's communist witch hunts, JFK's ill-conceived Cuban invasion and America's's disastrous involvement in Vietnam. Fulbright was truly a great American with unusual foresight about America's role to come as WWII had finally wound down but being replaced by the Cold War with Russia.

Sen. Fulbright saw that the one thing the devastated European countries still had were their higher learning institutions, their world renowned universities. He understood that newly discharged American soldiers could avail themselves of the opportunity to get a European university degree at costs to them far lower than in US based institutions (tuition in Europe was just about free). So, he said to the European education authorities: "Let our ex-GIs study in your universities and we will consider this as partial re-payment for the help we have given you." Thus was born the Fulbright Scholarship program - for American GI to study in Europe, an extension to the already well established study programs under the US 'GI Bill.' I remember quite a few of those US ex-soldiers in my engineering classes.

We envied the ex-GIs for their care-free demeanor exuding their pride of the victor. They had ample reason to enjoy their time at our universities, free of the pressing needs that ruled our days. With their ample supply of food and their cars they were getting all the girls they ever could want. We were poor and had to keep our minds on just making it to graduation. At least we did not have to fear them as competitors for our future jobs in Germany. Most of these GIs longed to go back to their home towns and their high school sweethearts. In any event, both the Fulbright and the GI Bill programs were hugely successful, not only because it afforded tens of thousands of young Americans a university education but also showed them that not everything in Europe was bad, the sad state of the university facilities notwithstanding.

In the early fifties, prompted largely by the political necessities of the Cold War, the Fulbright program was extended in the reverse direction, inviting European students to study in America, at US taxpayers' cost. This was not just generosity - it was meant to show young Europeans the many good sides of the American 'way of life' and to keep Europe's future leaders from falling for Communism's devious promises. For all these good reasons the Fulbright program became a resounding success. It was as a very enlightened way to spread American ideals in the world-wide competition with other ideologies. Seventy years later, at the time I am writing about it, the Fulbright program is still very much alive, and for the same good reasons.

We all knew, of course, of the simmering conflicts between the West and the Communist East. Living right at this fearsome fault line we Germans more than anyone else in this world were acutely aware how easily the world might explode any day into another catastrophic war. Getting an opportunity to step away from all that was great even if only for a year, but even greater was my exhilaration at getting to see the outside world, and of all places, America. There was no hesitation any more about all the unknown that I would be facing, not even the break in my budding academic career. My professor did extract my promise to return after my Fulbright year.

With great expectations of entering a new phase in my life I said good-bye to my parents. They were sad to see me go so far away but happy for my opportunity to begin to see the world that had been closed to most of us for so long.

I sailed from Rotterdam on a converted C-freighter serving then as a ship for refugees and American exchange students. Even by standards of those days this was a small ship with only rudimentary accommodations, and hopelessly overcrowded. It was the smallest of the 'US Liberty Ship' models that had been built in a hurry by the hundreds during the war. They had a reputation of not lasting very long - the calculation was that most of them would be sunk anyway before they would break down naturally, not very confidence-inspiring. As a newly minted engineer I noticed some rather interesting details - C-freighters were shallow draft vessels designed to enter small harbors or to get as close as possible to beaches. They had only one single old-fashioned piston steam engine fed by a single boiler and one single propeller -

no redundancy to fall back on in case of a failure.

The Atlantic crossing was scheduled to take ten days. The first part was like a dream. I had never seen the ocean - blue waters, balmy late summer days spent on deck with college students returning from their summer in Europe. You could not get much sleep at night, too much comings and goings in the dormitories. Needless to say, there was much fun to be had. We European Fulbright students were in great demand, a novelty for the American students, for some of them sometimes an unexpected opportunity for condescension and outright shows of prejudice - like "all Germans are....". But we did have a great time.

Suddenly the weather changed. On the last leg of our journey hurricane Hazel hit. Like everybody else I had experienced bad storms before but never on the high seas. Our ship rolled and heaved for three days, the bow flooded with every new wave crashing over. Every so often the stern and the ship's propeller would be lifted out of the water and for a moment the steam engine would speed up out of control

making the ship shudder as if breaking apart. Practically everybody got seasick. We were told not to get up on deck for fear of being swept overboard but we did anyway to escape the darkness, the stifling heat and the stench down below. The sea was churning, the wind howling and drenching the deck with rain and cold seawater.

Once I had gotten over the early signs of getting seasick I found this spectacle exhilarating, the wind whipping up the waves so that there was no line any more between water and the air. It was like a baptism by the wildness of the ocean. What a way to approach America!

A few days late our battered ship docked in Hoboken, New Jersey, on September 4, 1954. My new life in America had begun.

<O>

Phases of our Lives

AMERICA

"The American Dream is about Freedom"

- Nancy Pelosi

Phases of our Lives

America - My first Impressions

America! What were my first impressions? What did I make of all this new places, its people and how I would fit into it? From all I had been told I did think of America as "the world's last best hope", as Abraham Lincoln had put it a hundred years earlier.

What would my first impressions be, and how would those first impressions be lasting, or whether and how would they be revised after many years of living here? These are fundamental questions for all newcomers, no matter where and when. And I was very much aware of the idea that "other Nations are defined by their history, but America is mainly defined by its future", as Alexander Hamilton once had said. Would my coming experience here bear out this belief in America's exceptionalism?

Our ship had reached the entry to New York harbor at daybreak. We were all crowding the railings in awe at the first sight of the Manhattan skyline growing out of the morning haze. Passing the Statue of Liberty, Ellis Island and the docks of Staten Island and Brooklyn we marveled at the vastness of New York harbor bustling with ships of all sizes, from little tenders to huge ocean liners. We ever so slowly made it to our dock in Hoboken.

Heart beating in my chest I walked down the gangway from the ship into the cavernous pier structure. A bunch of rough looking stevedores were hustling our baggage. Long lines for immigration and customs. And a health check. The inspectors were stern but not unpleasant. They were very thorough - entering the United States at that time was a really big deal. After all, the entire world wanted to get here, and there had to be strict controls, otherwise the nation would have been overrun with millions seeking a place of peace and freedom - and a chance to get away from misery and oppression in the 'Old Country.'

Of course I had been used to equally strict border controls between European countries. But I was soon to learn that there was a huge difference: after we had passed immigration and customs and set foot onto American soil there were no controls any more of any kind! At that time, in Europe, wherever you would go there always would be on-going controls everywhere. For example, to move to another town you needed a permit and upon arrival you had to register at the police station. Here for the first time I experienced the exhilarating sensation of Freedom!

Someone with a big cardboard sign with the letters "IIE" greeted us Fulbrighters. He was a guide sent on behalf of the 'Institute of International Education' which was officially commissioned with taking care of Fulbrighters. We followed him out of the pier building, down a flight of stairs into the underground train station (the 'Tubes' as it was called then, connecting Hoboken with mid-town Manhattan), and off we went. We had been told that this train would go underneath the Hudson and leave us off at our Manhattan hotel were we would stay for a few days of 'orientation.'

After a fifteen minute ride through the darkness of the tunnel the train stopped and we were walking through another tunnel. Up a flight of stairs we found ourselves - surprise! - in the lobby of the Hotel Martinique. From the moment we had entered the train in Hoboken to us registering in the hotel lobby we had not seen daylight - the marvels of the big city underground! Today you take this type of thing as normal but imagine how astounding it was in the eyes of a newcomer.

Then it suddenly hit us that it was terribly hot, an ever present stifling humid heat that none of us Northern Europeans had ever experienced. We had been told that New York would be hot in Summer and frightfully cold in Winter, but this heat! It was especially hard for us to take, as none of us had the right clothing. We were still wearing our woolen sports coats and necktie. The hotel was old, no air conditioning. The street did not give any relief. We now understood: we had arrived in the aftermath of hurricane

Hazel which had pummeled our ship and then, a few days later, New York.

We had arrived on a Saturday. Manhattan overwhelmed us with its sky scrapers, the incessant traffic, the screaming subways, the parks, and above all the never ending movements of people. We had, of course, heard about all that but the reality of being there was something else. But what hit us the most was the apparent friendliness and the ready smiles on just about everyone we met in those first days. In Europe at that time many people were still sullen and not ready yet to give up their deep mistrust of everyone else.

We also found out that we had arrived on one of the most important holiday weekends - Labor Day. This gave us also Monday to explore the city before our 'orientation' would start in the IIE. It gave me time to look up one of Father's Jewish friends who had left Germany just in time to save himself and his family from the Nazi prosecution. Mustering all my courage I went down and hailed a taxi. Clambering in I was trying to find the piece of paper with the address. Impatiently the taxi driver turned around and barked at me "where to, *Mac*?" I was stunned: how in the world would this man know my name? Dark thoughts raced through my German mind: Wow, they were tracking me here after all! Am I under surveillance? It took me some time to realize that obviously that was not so - addressing someone as 'Mac' was just a common thing, especially for a New York taxi driver. No, people were not being tracked here.

It turned out that my visit to this family was not welcome. My father's friend had long since passed away and his family had no use for anything German. It was my first encounter with such strong anti-German sentiments. There would be a lot more to come. It was as if all of a sudden a big 'caution' sign had appeared. After all, a good number of Americans were still of the belief that all Germans were guilty for the war and the unspeakable crimes committed in the name of Germany. It would take many more years until this idea of Germany's 'Collective Guilt' would make place of a more nuanced understanding of the fact that Germany was not the monolithic place of evil that the war propaganda had crated in the minds of so many Americans.

But this would not make me lose the sense of exhilaration of being given such a wonderful opportunity to learn all about America, the land of so many of my dreams. In many ways this sobering encounter made me more aware of the complexity of America and its people. It also prepared me to see more than the surface of life in America, to be more sensitive to its rich diversity as well as to the problems it was wrestling with. All this served me well when later on I would be confronted with issues of race, religions and other elements of American life that were new to me.

But then things turned much brighter. As a part of getting to know Americans away from academia the IIE had arranged host families. To be invited into their homes and offered genuine hospitality was a pleasant surprise to me. Remember that in those days in Europe people were still very reserved, to say the least. Years of oppression had firmly engrained a great distrust of anyone outside their inner circles. People there preferred to stay to themselves.

It was so refreshing for me to be welcomed with open arms and invited into the homes of people I had never met before. To be trusted even as we were foreigners! That would never have happened in Europe where people were still reeling from destruction and mistrust. But I was a bit confused about all the assumptions that our American hosts had made about the reasons why we Fulbrighters were in America. In those days it was apparently taken for granted that everyone coming to America would be some kind of refugee in distress hoping to get help to build a new life. No, I was not a refugee, and I had all the intention to go back to Germany, in spite of all the hardships that people like us had to endure. I felt uncomfortable when they would heap their compassion and pity a bit too thick in their eagerness to show us their welcoming side. They all meant so well. We wanted to make sure that they would not be disappointed.

Just about everyone I met outside academia seemed surprised that I had come as a post-graduate scholar already equipped with a full university education. It seemed strange to them that I was not even planning to stay here but to return to Germany at the end of my Fulbright year. Some even were a even bit disappointed that I would not fully turn away from my home country - they were so convinced that America was the only place where anyone would want to live, ever. They had good reason to be proud of their country. Nothing in the world came close to their generosity and their willingness to help those in need. And justly they would tell us with pride about the freedom that Americans enjoyed.

It is the idea of Freedom that defines America best. Americans have indeed achieved an unprecedented degree of personal freedom that is the envy of the rest of the world. That was especially true for us post-war Europeans who were still accustomed to controls about just every decision a normal person would want to make. You can define 'Freedom' in at least two ways: Freedom of choice what to do, what to buy, how to entertain yourself and - most important - how and where to make your living. We were in awe of the ease with which Americans felt free to voice their opinions even the most controversial matters. In its pure form the 'Freedom of Choice' concept leaves each person on their own in dealing with life's risks. It is very much reflected in the American ideal of total self-sufficiency. Some think that this way of looking at 'Freedom' also leads to an over-emphasis of measuring the standard of living by how much people can buy with what they earn.

Truth is that unlike so many newcomers to America, the abundance of food and other material things did not much impress me. I had grown up with a lot of hunger, deprivation and the obvious longing for more comforts but I was always uncomfortable when newcomers to America would be looking agape at the over-abundance of goods and the reckless consumption. To me, this was not what America was all about - I was much more drawn to the broader concept of Freedom defined by the absence of oppression, within a well functioning legal system for the protection of personal safety, with easy access to education and help for the sick and old age.

To me, the essence of Freedom was the idea that the State would not be able to dictate life styles, and removing much of the fear about those parts of our lives that we cannot control. Removing the element of fear in everybody's life is at the core of personal freedom, a dream for us Europeans after our disastrous experiences with war and dictatorships. But in the end, perhaps, somewhere in the scheme of things, there actually may be a connection between

Freedom and the astounding and wide-spread prosperity in America.

Many asylum seekers are fleeing oppression and fears for their personal safety in their home country for the 'Freedoms' of America. Some of them, however, were in reality coming here just for what they saw as easy living without much of a will to make their own contributions. Much of the widespread resentments by many Americans against this type of immigrant comes from this basic misinterpretation of what 'Freedom' really means.

My idea of Freedom was always on a different plane - I saw Freedom as the result of having taken the right to make decisions on our personal lives away from the State and putting it into the hands of the individual citizen. Of course this type of 'Freedom' only works if all citizens take the full responsibility for their decisions and actions. Those who came to America without understanding this would run the risk of not truly becoming comfortable with their newly found Freedom which indeed set America apart from the Europe of my days.

Ultimately my concept of Freedom was that of the thinkers of the Enlightenment, foremost my all-time favorite poet and playwright Friedrich Schiller. His timeless poem "Ode to Joy," put to glorious music by his friend Beethoven would become treasured by the entire world. In his original version, Schiller actually meant to say "Ode to Freedom" but that was going too far in those days of repressive censorship. To young Germans he personified the idea of personal freedom, *"the precious right to elect our own duties"* - exactly my concept of what 'freedom' is, or should be, all about..

Schiller celebrated this most personal concept of Freedom in his down-to-earth plays and wonderfully rhymed ballads that many of us had to learn by heart - and we loved every minute of it. In his plays he would courageously confront the despotic rulers of his days (in the early 1800s) and as a result he found himself imprisoned once.

Back from his prison, Schiller continued his rebellious writings. His hallmark play, "The Robbers" was a sort of Robin Hood theme but aiming not at taking from the rich to help the poor but protecting those unjustly persecuted. Freedom and Justice were his themes. In an attempt to stay clear of the censors he put his provocative writings into the distant past especially in his drama "Don Carlos" - just like Shakespeare had done before him, for the the same reasons.. Needless to say, the Nazis would ban Schiller's works - to no avail. Their book-burning had made Schiller even more popular to us young Germans, albeit in secret.

Freedom in America is the envy of the world (at least in its civilized parts). It would do a lot of good for everybody interested in the concept of personal freedom to read Schiller's works - you would be surprised how direct and clearly he addressed this fundamental human issue, almost two hundred years ago now. It also makes very entertaining reading!

But I was not sent to America to wax philosophically about its uniqueness, its freedom, however defined. I was sent here to spent a year at an American university, under my Fulbright scholarship. And the underlying expectation was that, like the many other Fulbright scholars, we would learn to appreciate America and embrace its values, not what the European communists were trying to tell us. We were very much aware that we, in a way, were pawns in the epic struggle between the forces of oppression and collectivism, and the personal freedom offered by the West.

Needless to say I was apprehensive about what I would find in my coming ten months in American academia. Would it be all that I was told to expect?

I was ready. Or so I thought.

Phases of our Lives

Finding my Way into American Academia

"Things are different here."
Prof. Appleby, Syracuse University's Dean of Students,
welcoming us Fulbright students.

On our first Tuesday morning in New York our 'orientation' started in the IIE's grand mansion on 65th Street. I knew I was assigned to Syracuse University - I never learned why but it would turn out to be just the right place for me. I had already received a welcome letter from the Syracuse Dean of Students, Dean Appleby. Just the idea to receive a welcome letter from a university official was a surprise to me. In his letter Dean Appleby was being a bit chummy - among other fatherly advise he suggested to bring "woolen underwear because winters in upstate New York tend to be cold." Well well, that is thoughtful, but perhaps a bit personal. On top, does he really think that we post-war Germans had such a luxury as woolen underwear? What other lack of understanding of our conditions of life in post-war Germany would I encounter?

One more day of leisure in New York and then off to Syracuse, by train, along the breathtaking Hudson valley, in its glorious Fall colors. The school had already assigned me to a graduate student building where I shared a three bedroom apartment with a student from India and an ex-GI from New York. So far everything had worked like a charm. And the 'campus'! Gorgeous English-college style buildings set in beautifully landscaped hills, enormous trees in full fall splendor - a dream compared with the drab utilitarian universities of Germany, like Karlsruhe, in 1954 much of it still in ruins.

There were still a few days before school would open. I roamed the Syracuse city streets and admired the abundance of trees everywhere, especially in the living areas. From a hill side overlook you could barely see any buildings for all the majestic trees - the town looked more like a forest to me. The leafs were still on, but many branches were down because the remains of Hazel had swept right through the city. It was still hot, very hot. I began to wonder whether Dean Appleby had known that when he was talking about Syracuse being so cold in winter. I would find out soon enough.

Finally the day of 'registration' had come. I marched up the few blocks to the administration building, an English manor style brick structure perched up on a hill. The campus, totally empty until that day, was now teeming with hundreds of students. Somehow they did not seem to move around much - they all stood in some line - lines for class registrations, one for each department, lines for housing, one for sports, lines for all kinds of clubs, one for an 'advisor' and so on... I had no idea where to go and I had no interest to stand in any line - I had my fill of this standing in line during and after the war. I simply could not understand why there were so many things to do about something as basic as getting students started in their studies. I would find out soon enough why this was so.

In my German university experience we would simply go to the administration, pick up a registration booklet, enter the courses we knew we had to take to eventually graduate, and that was it. No standing in line. If you wanted sports, you went where they played and joined in. If you wanted a club you went to their meetings. As far as housing, you fended for yourself. The difference was not that the administrations of German universities were smarter. One difference was that when you entered a German university you were older - mostly 20 or 21, and you were expected to know how to deal with the logistics of a higher education life. In America, coming out of high school at age 17 or 18 and usually from a very protective environment you could not really expect the level of maturity needed to figure out all these requirements without someone telling you what to do. I turned 25 while at Syracuse, obviously way above the average age of students there, and I thought I was already used to fend for myself.

For students in American colleges it is of course wonderful to have so many programs and facilities available to them. It makes American schools unique because their great emphasis on activities beyond the basic academics makes their students much more socially adept. So much socializing, especially among the undergraduates! I began to wonder when they actually did their studying. It seemed to me that everything was done to make their college life a happy experience. One result was a rather superficial learning with a lot less work input than what was expected at European schools. Much later I learned that in undergraduate studies most students spent less than one hour per day on home work - compared with at least four hours for us. Our European schools didn't give a hoot whether we were happy or not. They would load us up with so much work that too often even the most studious ones would break. With that heavy a work load we could never afford to spend anywhere near as much time with sports and partying.

It astounded me how many non-teaching people were employed by American schools. Of course, for all these extra-curricular activities there had to be people to administer them, offices for just about everything a student may want to do, with endless forms to be filled out - often you had to stand in line just to get the forms!

As an example from my own 'Alma Maters', today Syracuse has 23,000 students with 1,600 teachers and 5,700 non-teaching staff, or 3 staff employees to each teacher. In Karlsruhe there are 21,000 students with 6,000 teaching positions and 3,400 staff, or half a staff member for each teacher. It shows clearly the relative emphasis on studying vs. making sure the students are having a good time.

A big part of this indulgence in non-teaching activities is the outsized attention given to college team sports. It is often said that these team sports bring in a lot of money. After a lifetime in management I am accustomed to examine the true costs of operations, and I have seen too often how managers fall for the temptation to make their departments look good by 'creative' accounting, like charging big parts of their true costs to other activities, or to 'overhead'. These large sports programs are 'sacred cows' and no one wants to face the truth that most of them probably are in fact a financial drain on the school when you consider everything, like the cost of stadiums, the travels of hundreds of team members and their hangers-on, and on and on.

If it were true that college sports bring in so much money, why then are American colleges so expensive? It certainly cannot be because of the very meager salaries of their professors. How about the many hundreds of 'students' on athletic scholarships in each of our sports-crazy schools who collect handsome stipends, being coddled all along with meaningless courses to finish with a sham 'degree'? What does it say about our educational priorities when our college sports coaches make more than ten times as much money as the most sought-after professors?

But guess - we Europeans did enjoy these nice amenities immensely.

Sometimes we Fulbrighters had to bite our tongues when we had to listen to condescending statements about the countries we had come from. Even in academic circles many Americans found it difficult to understand that not everything in the 'old country' was without merit. For them, there was only one possible way of life - the American one, and it was difficult for them to understand that each country, each nation, had its own history, had to grow its own civic culture, and had to learn to live with it.

Getting to know America's Ways

Naturally we foreign student were quite popular on campus but more as a curiosity. When I came to America my English was quite good already - after nine years of Gymnasium and the translation work I had done at Karlsruhe. But, like any other language, English can trip you up with double meanings and plays with words ("*There is no time like the present to present you with the present of my book*").

For example, in one of the numerous forms we had to fill out there was this question "Do you drink?" I was perplexed. Does not everybody drink, like water, tea or milk? I had been totally unaware that Syracuse at that time was a Methodist sponsored university and therefor adamant about alcohol. So, cheerfully, I answered this question with a clear and unqualified "yes". Looking at my questionnaire my 'advisor' raised her eyebrows, looked at me but then let it go. The truth, of course, was that Syracuse students were indeed 'drinking' and often to an excess I had not seen even in German fraternities. It opened my eyes to a lot of strange discrepancies between what was said officially and what was being practiced in reality.

There was a lot of confusion about the European educational system and how we could meet the 'prerequisites' for any of the graduate courses I wanted to take. I showed them the records from my graduate studies at the 'Karlsruhe Technische Hochschule' as it was called then (now a full university). The idea that the "TH Karlsruhe' could be considered to be in the same league as MIT or CalTech did not resonate. The words 'Technische Hochschule' got stuck in everybody's throat. They simply translated it into their understanding of an American 'Technical High School', and no amount of explaining would move them away from their fixed ideas.

I was ready to throw up my hands trying to explain the differences between the European and the American educational structures. But then I had an idea: I saw that there were quite a few faculty and students who did want to know about this issue and so I offered to give a seminar on this subject. Contributing something to the school in addition to just taking courses was sort of expected from Fulbright scholars so I did not think I would be out of bounds with my suggestion. I was called in to present my case to the faculty. Had I been too presumptuous? After the usual deliberations they agreed to let me do it and from there on treated me like a 'de facto' member of the Syracuse faculty - sort of.

So I started my seminar. To my surprise, my class room filled up quickly. I knew I had to be careful in the way I was to express my views. I certainly did not want to come across as negative on American views and institutions. And - god forbid - I surely did not want ever to be viewed as some sort of Nazi. It was bad enough that some of the faculty and probably a few student were not at all comfortable having a young German among them, given the horrors that they or their parents had to endure before finding the comfort and safety of America. Here is a brief outline of my seminar:

"Underlying the American educational system is the idea of extending the concept of social equality into the world of education. In theory this is meant to give every young person the same teaching curriculum. In real life, of course, in most American schools students are given different levels of teaching according to ability just like in the European system and, admit it or not, according to socio-economic background. American schools are well known to be superior to the European in their development of their students' independent thinking, their social skills, and of course in their emphasis of athletics.

Against these uncontested advantages of the American system it is difficult to argue about the benefits of the European one. Americans think it inconsistent with the idea of equality to separate students at the young age of ten into those who remain in elementary school (destined to learn a trade) and the ten percent or so of higher performers who are admitted to the eight or nine years of higher learning in secondary schools (about one third of these are then destined for university). Let us not use the term 'high school' for this secondary level - European secondary schools typically include the equivalent of about two years of American college.

As to school management, American schools offer many 'hand-holding' amenities that are generally unavailable in Europe, like the office of student counseling, of registration, of transcripts, of fraternities and sports, even the 'Dean of Students.' All these offerings and activities help making American student much more socially adept than their European counterparts.

In the European system the emphasis is almost exclusively on academics, to a point where studying is taking just about all time available with untold hours of homework. Therefore the time-honored American idea of 'working your way through college' is just about impossible in Europe. In addition most European students spend more days at school - about 230 days per year vs. probably less than 170 days in most American schools, counting vacations, the many official holidays and the 'special days' like teachers conference etc. The long three months summer vacations possibly can make many American students forget some of what they had learned in the past semesters but it allows them to take summer jobs, or to enrich their learning through social, cultural or athletic activities and travel. These opportunities are rarely available to European students.

Another important difference is the frequency of testing. In America it is normal to have many tests, often weekly 'quizzes', with the emphasis on moving on to a new subject to be tested in another week or so. It allows American colleges to cover more material in a given time. European students are expected to study for the acquisition of permanent knowledge that would be tested a lot less frequently, sometimes once a year only, putting the emphasis on developing long term memory skill.

One striking example of the difference in schooling is the concept that in European schools at all levels the curriculum is unified country-wide and has to meet State administered minimum levels of acquired knowledge, and this is strictly enforced. As a result, when you graduate, your Diploma would be your license to practice in the field of your studies - graduating from engineering school entitled you to practice engineering, graduating from law school to practice law, from medical school to practice medicine etc. In America, lacking a unified minimum country-wide standard for graduating, you have to pass additional exams to become a licensed 'professional engineer', or to pass the 'boards' to become licensed to practice law or medicine, separately for each state of the Union (as if the laws of physics, the principles of engineering or the medical procedures could be any different in each State).

The lack of unified minimum achievements in American higher education is ultimately the legacy of the Jeffersonian concept of government - delegating decision-making to the lowest level of community. As a result every little school board in every little town in America is expected to make decisions on what is to be taught, how it is to be taught, and what books to use, much to the delight of the text book sellers who are making billions selling gullible school boards on the outrageous idea that they have to buy new textbooks every year, as if physics, chemistry, English and even history would change every year.

In Jefferson's days, this local decision making idea may have made some sense, considering the primitive communication and travel conditions in those days. To keep this outdated method alive in today's global competition is, mildly put, an anachronism, but so dear to the hearts of our school boards and PTAs.

This antiquated concept has resulted in some quite confusing situations - for example, every one in America can call himself an 'engineer' - the guy who runs the train is called 'engineer', the handyman in your building is the 'building engineer', and so on. No wonder there is a need for separate 'professional' licensing exams in America.

But much more important, and in a nut shell: European academics (at any level) concentrate almost exclusively on strictly standardized academics - to a fault, grossly neglecting the needs of young people to develop social skills and independent thinking. By contrast the American way sometimes gives the development of social skills and student initiatives priority over pure academics, perhaps at the expense of conveying actual language and science skills.

What is the better way? In their own way, both systems are producing excellent graduates. One of the many possible criteria to judge the 'pros and cons' was so well put by the renowned education critic, W. Deresiewicz:

"The central intellectual ability you are supposed to acquire in college is that of the ability to analyze other people's arguments and then formulate your own."

By that definition, which system would be the winner?"

Well, we know that both systems turn out excellent graduates. In both systems it definitely depends solely on the will and the ability of the students to embrace the unique opportunities given to them to prepare them for their later lives.

In any event, my seminars on higher education, here and there, turned out quite successful, being attended more by faculty than by students. What I liked most about it was their lively participation, asking questions without any hesitation and even challenging some of my points, something totally unheard-of in my Karlsruhe experience. The products of American schools are definitely more self-assured and not afraid to speak up. Did I make a dent in their still prevailing prejudices? I will never know, but it made my year at Syracuse a lot more meaningful to me.

Without question, teaching at the Syracuse engineering school was indeed of the highest level. I could have learned a lot. At that time the Americans were ahead of the Europeans in chemical plant design, especially in the theoretic analysis part. What threw me off was the way the classes were being conducted - to us European students it was like being back at Gymnasium: roll calls, daily or weekly 'quizzes', many in a 'multiple choice' format. No wonder - even in the graduate courses many students were very young and somewhat immature, obviously not being trusted by their professors that they would do the work unless prodded daily.

Right or wrong, I did not like this throw-back to my 'high school' days. So I made a bold decision: Instead of going deeper into my chemical engineering I opted to do something entirely different - I enrolled in the Business School to get a Master of Business degree. Dean Appleby came through and paved my way for this unusual request.

I had always had an interest in the management aspect of engineering. As a part of the requirements at Karlsruhe for my advanced engineering degree I had to take basic law, finance and management courses. After the usual discussions the Syracuse Maxwell School of Business gave me credit for enough basic courses to make it possible for me to get my MBA in the nine months left on my scholarship deal. It was hard work. They doubted that I would be able to do this, especially language-wise, but my nine years of English at Gymnasium and the translation work I had done at Karlsruhe came in handy. I just made it for the End of May graduation. My thesis was on "The Emergence of Petroleum as Raw Material for Chemicals Production," a subject that was of great interest at that time as oil was about to replace coal as the preferred

starting material for the basic building blocks of industrial chemistry. An abstract of my thesis was printed in the "Chemical Engineering" magazine. I had become a published author in America!

For the graduation ceremony I borrowed the required gown from a friend, not wanting to spend my precious dollars on the graduation pageantry which I thought to be an anachronism and a bit out of place in modern day America - faculty in traditional English garb, carrying mace, scepter and other medieval symbols. Only much later did I come to understand its psychological significance, making the conclusion of university studies so much more memorable to the departing students. It also probably helped to loosen the graduates parents' purse strings for donations to the schools' endowments, something quite foreign to European universities which are mainly state funded. In the many animated discussions on these world view matters I learned quickly to become very cautious not to step on peoples' toes unnecessarily - and the ideology of the educational systems is certainly one of the sensitive areas that reflect the very basic concepts of who should determine what is to be taught and how to do it.

In the end, what did I come away with from my year in American academia? Obviously there was a lot to be learned. For me it was not a matter of finding out what is better or what is worse in the European and the American way. When you come to a new country you can make the decision to embrace all its habits and beliefs and shed your old ones. I opted not to take this path. I looked at my American experiences as an addition to what my home country had given me, not its replacement, but rather an incredibly valuable enrichment.

In any event, I knew that I would spend one year in this country and then return to my home to resume my academic career. After all, I had not come to America as a refugee, not with the plan to stay here, not even to start getting an education. To my great relief my Karlsruhe professor was not angry with me for having chosen to get an MBA instead of deepening my ChemE. He was ready to take me back and to help me with my academic career. He even thought that my having acquired an MBA would actually be a good thing for eventually getting a professorship. So, my road to the coveted academic career had remained open for me.

But then, with one single question, all of that would change - once again.

Phases of our Lives

Phases of our Lives

MAKING MY LIVING

Phases of our Lives

My Career Begins in Earnest

I had noticed him taking his seat in the back of the seminar room. He was not a 'regular' and a bit older than most of the students but not faculty either. I saw he was not taking notes but was obviously paying close attention. After I had dismissed the class he came up to me and said:

"Would you like to do a one year engineering and management training with us?"

He was Gene Winnie, Executive Vice President of W.R.Grace's newly formed Chemicals Division. What little I knew about W.R.Grace & Co ('Grace' for short) was that it was one of the most prestigious and fastest growing groups of companies based in New York, with plants all over the world. Why would his company make such an offer? Winnie simply said that like other American industries his company offered one-year internships as some form of continued education to deserving graduate students. If I would accept, they would send me to some of their plants in the US to get an exposure to American engineering and plant management practices, no strings attached, with a small stipend to cover living expenses.

Who would not want to accept this offer for another year in America learning more of the practical side of engineering and plant operations?

But making the decision to accept this offer was not that easy. What would my Prof. Kirschbaum think of this new change of plans? Would he keep my spot in his department open for yet another year? To my great relief he said "Yes." In fact he encouraged me to make the best use of this unique opportunity to add practical American experience to my academics.

That made it easy for me to accept Grace's offer. I still had to tell my family - no problem there, of course. They were missing me, they said, but what an opportunity, on top of it all!

First, a few weeks of getting to know each other at the Grace headquarters, in the famed New York financial district, in the Cotton Exchange Building on Hanover Square - very prestigious and a bit overwhelming for me, the wide-eyed greenhorn from a little town in Germany. Looking back, I must assume that the Grace people were wondering what their colleague Gene Winnie had brought into their lofty executive suite. Somehow I did get their nod, and off I was to my first assignment: Grace's brand new ammonia fertilizer plant in Memphis, Tennessee

What a stroke of luck! After all, at Karlsruhe I had worked in Prof. Haber's laboratory, the very place where this nitrogen fixation process had been developed! It made me an instant expert in the eyes of the Memphis plant operators. I went to work as a special assistant to the plant manager, John Carriere, a dyed-in-the-wool Southerner with an aristocratic air about him. We got along very well. The plant itself was a few miles north of the city, in the middle of seemingly endless cotton fields. I bought my first car, a ten year old beautiful big black Buick which I drove around happy as a lark.

The best part of being Carriere's protegé was an easy entry into some of the old Memphis families who were thrilled to show me off to their friends as their 'European visitor'. With his introduction I found an apartment - not just any apartment, the 'carriage house' behind a grand city mansion (in the good old days, the slave quarters). This was the type of place that would be rented to 'proper' young men who were expected to be fitting in with the local gentry. I could not believe my good fortune. The masters of this mansion, Mr. and Mrs. Powers, were the arch-image of southerners ruling over their black servants with dignified authority. They were wealthy, childless, and taking in renters like me gave them the company of 'proper' young men almost as a substitute for being childless. They showered me with kindness, inviting me frequently to dine with them and most important introduced me to a few girls. I had it made!

But this was the American South. There was strict separation from the blacks who were the majority - separate in everything, in restaurants, at water fountains and even in churches. I had been warned to be careful and not do or say anything that would be 'inappropriate.' That did not prevent me from being perplexed. How could that be in a modern country, in America, that prides itself that "all men are created equal"? Well, it was not my place to rock that boat. Naturally I saw this racial tension with the eyes of one that just had come from Germany where the most heinous crimes had been committed in the name of racial purity. Some would be quick to say that there was a huge difference - in Germany these race crimes had been sanctioned, in fact ordained, by the state, whereas the mistreatment and even the lynchings of negroes in America were done by the 'free' acts of individuals. My contention was that for the hapless victim hanging from a tree it made little difference - for him or her the suffering was the same.

What did irk me was the Southerners' frequently overt hypocrisy. My landlady presented me with an excellent example. During one of the many gracious dinners she started talking about the many problems that she thought the South had with its negroes, with their laziness, their lack of morals, their inability to learn and their civic irresponsibilities. It did not seem to bother her that all this was said in the presence of her negro servants. As I had been instructed, I made no comment. She then proceeded to tell us that God in his infinite wisdom had arranged it so that the negroes were becoming less black with every new generation. You see, she said, now that they lived in our moderate climate they no longer needed the black pigment in their skin that in Africa had been necessary to protect them from the burning African sun..... I am still not quite sure what went on in her mind. Was she really unaware of the never-to-be acknowledged fact that more and more blacks had babies with whites? Was it just a coded way of acknowledging reality? To me it was just hypocrisy, plain and simple.

This strange denial of simple everyday realities showed up everywhere in the South, especially in relations with Southern girls. They were, of course, as interested in boys - and sex - as any healthy young person and they would do the same things that normal young people do - but all along making these pious announcements that they would never lower themselves to give in to temptation. It would confuse me to no end.

But altogether my six months in Memphis were good for me. I began to understand more about America and especially its Southern parts. I learned a lot about plant engineering and how to get the plant operators to do what I saw as the right engineering practices. It helped that I was perceived by them as the big boss's 'fair-haired boy' but it also drove home the point that unless I could assert my authority on my own I would not get more than lip service. This, perhaps, was the most important lesson from my Memphis stay.

My next assignment was Grace's new plastics plant in Baton Rouge, Louisiana. After the rather cosmopolitan Memphis, Baton Rouge was the petrochemical 'hinterlands,' and the plant itself was not even finished. My job was to assist plant management in preparing the start-up, section by section, together with a handful of other young engineers fresh out of college. Our schedule was typical for this task: three of four days of almost 24 hours intensive work, and then a week or so off, until the next plant section was to be made ready. This was great - it allowed us to explore exotic Louisiana, starting with navigating the romantic but also dangerous bayous (the often menacing natives speak a kind of adulterated French) to the excitement of New Orleans' night life.

Sometimes we would complain to our red-neck plant manager about our dismal social life, and more than once he tried to make us go out with his secretary. She was pretty alright but not very bright, and we would say to him that "you can't even talk to that girl." His down-to-earth response:"Who wants to talk!"

America, even its deep South, began to be less of an enigma to me. I began to feel comfortable there and more self-assured. These 'apprenticeships' were good for me.

Learning to make the big Decisions

At that time plastics as an industrial product were new to America and still considered chemical curiosities. Now the mass production of these new materials was beginning. Grace's plant was designed to produce a new version of 'High Density Polyethylene' developed originally in Germany and improved by Phillips Petroleum of Bartlesville in Oklahoma. To be with a totally new technology was exciting, the dream of many aspiring leaders in engineering.

When I started working there I had no idea that it would become my field of work for many years as an engineer, manager and business partner. These were truly 'pioneering days' in a brand new industry. It was to be my destiny.

Of course, I did not know that yet at the time. Instead, as my one year as Grace's intern was about to come to its end I was getting busy packing for my return to Germany. Prof.Kirschbaum was expecting me back in Karlsruhe to resume my work as Assistant Professor in his Chemical Engineering department.

And once more, my plans were changed. I had been invited back to Grace's New York headquarters for what I thought would be a 'de-briefing' after my year as their intern. Gene Winnie sat me down in his office overlooking New York harbor, the Statue of Liberty at a distance in the morning haze. After just a little chit-chat ("how did you like Memphis...") he came straight out: "We would like to offer you a job as our technical liaison man for our European plastics companies."

Wow. Speechless once more.

It became clear to me only then that my year as intern was in fact a way for Grace to see whether I would indeed be of value to them for their new presence in Europe. Making good use of the high value of the US dollar at that time Grace had acquired a number of European companies who then were at the forefront of the emerging plastics technology. Grace needed multilingual young engineers who knew their way around Europe and would help manage these companies. Such a set of qualifications was difficult to find among young Americans. In those days of border controls, visa requirements and still rough living conditions most Americans considered working in Europe a 'hardship' assignment. It was also the days of 'the Ugly American' that made many Europeans uncomfortable with some of the Americans that had started to travel and work abroad.

This is why Grace wanted to hire young European Fulbrighters to do their bidding in Europe. My job would be to transfer new plastics technologies between Grace divisions in the US, Europe and South America and to do the licensing of new technologies from the big European plastics companies. For this they needed young engineers that had the ability to deal with the European establishment on an equal professional and social footing.

How could I possibly turn down such an opportunity?

But what would Prof. Kirschbaum say to yet another change of plans? This time, he was not willing any more to keep my place open. With good justification he wrote me that he had supported me in two major decisions that took me away from his original plans for me. But as I was now taking a permanent position in industry I had in his view made my final decision not to pursue the German academic career. I was crushed - but really, could I keep that venue open indefinitely? Of course not, but I was determined to do lecturing and writing papers whenever I could. I was not turning back from the 'teacher' in me.

My parents were not happy with my decision. They still thought of me as a future German university professor. And they pointed out over and over that American companies were known to hire and fire people at will. German companies, and of course, German universities did not do that, ever. Jobs there were safe.

But I was young and job security was not high on my list - the adventure of being able to travel to different countries and being on the forefront of new technologies was.

Think of it: traveling all over Europe, and back and forth to America! This was 1956. At that time traveling like that was only for the 'rich and famous.' And staying in the very best hotels of the world! Rubbing shoulders with European industry leaders! Given the freedom to pretty much making my own work plans! And on top of all that getting paid in the almighty Dollar which in those days had enormous purchasing power all over the world!

Still I hesitated. I asked Father - he was skeptical: How can you rely on the free-wheeling Americans? Your future is here, in your native Germany! Yes, we had to go through an awful lot but this is your home! You owe a lot to your home country - it needs people like you!

I asked Mama - she would miss me terribly. Hold it, I said: With my freedom of travel I would probably be able see you more often than if I had a 'steady' job in an German university or industry. Sister Anneliese was excited for me: "What an opportunity for you!"

Of course, I took the job.

Phases of our Lives

The 'European Hand'

And it all came true - and much more. I would indeed 'roam the world', flying across the Atlantic to just about every country in Europe - and this at a time when that kind of traveling was very, very unusual. It was, after all, still the 1950's and early 1960's, with the world still in the grips of the Cold War. My languages came in very handy - not so many Europeans spoke English then. The 'Lingua Franca' of the educated class was still French, which suited me just fine. And, yes, I would meet the most interesting and powerful European industrialists and opened their doors to my New York bosses who loved every minute of it. I was on a roll. I had become W.R.Grace's 'European Hand,' living in grand style in the best hotels.

Grace's European head office was in London, on 98 Fenchurch Street, headed by Allan Beavis, an old-school British executive, later to be knighted for his international business successes (of which, in fact, I was not so small a part).

Sharing my modest office was Derek Dryden, the quintessential English accountant right out of Dickens. Having served as sergeant during the war he was very reserved toward me in the beginning but warmed up nicely, given his ram-rod soldierly being. He gave me a healthy respect for what the British then called "being good at sums"- the ability to add, subtract, multiply and divide English money. Sounds trite? Ha! Think of the British currencies of those days: one Guinea equals 21 Shillings, one Pound 20 Shillings, one Shilling 12 Pence, one Farthing... Just try! Now, of course, all this is metric, like anywhere else.

With his meticulous accounting he would keep track of my travels and my expenses. He taught me a very valuable lesson: the best way to judge a man's potential for management positions is his expense account - if you cheat on the expense account you will probably also cheat on your management duties.

I was given an assistant, John Harding, a typical British Public School boy, obviously from a good family with impeccable manners but very shy and initially easily overwhelmed - in his position as my anchor person he had to learn to take initiatives, something that was not a part at all of his up-bringing. Gradually I taught him how to track performance of the newly established licensees, specify and procure the materials they needed and learning to purchase raw materials. On special occasions, like industry conventions, I took him with me in my travels on the Continent which brought out in him the potential of an international trader which is what he aspired to all along. I lost track of him so I do not know whether he did indeed go in that direction. In any way, it was my first attempt to guide a young employee through a learning period that would create a sound basis for his future success. It was my first experience how good it felt to help a young man to find 'his groove' in my world of the technology business. There were many others to follow in my efforts to make them a success. It felt good to be able to do this.

London in the late 1950s was a great place. The scars of the war were still around us, but there was history everywhere, and of course Albert Hall, the British Museum and the innumerable play houses. And, yes, there was the infamous London Fog, so thick that even during daytime you could not see the person in front of you. I vividly remember one day when I opened the widow to let some air into our stuffy offices when I was met with an outcry:"don't let the fog come in!" It was quite a sight: the fog coming into the offices like a dense smoke. I also understood then why so many Englishmen seemed to be plagued by cases of perpetual nasal congestion!

From our London base I would travel all over Europe, using the Grace offices in Paris, Dusseldorf and Milan as my regional bases. My routine was to spend about six weeks back in New York for planning my work, and then six weeks or so roaming about Europe, and later on South America. In my job I had to find new technology that would be useful for the different Grace chemical and plastics operations and then negociating licensing agreements. I became good at sniffing out new technologies, products and processes and to teach our various divisions how to use them efficiently.

It was a dream job for a young engineer where I could put to use my talents: knowledge of technology, evaluating their economics, and honing my skills of 'selling' our division heads on their merit. My languages helped, and so did the 'teacher' in me. My Grace bosses in New York liked what I was doing. It seemed I was becoming indispensable to them as their 'European Hand', opening doors to the top managers of the emerging European plastics enterprises.

I could pretty much set my own schedule and therefore I could take time off whenever I wanted to visit my parents or sister Anneliese, or enjoy the sites. Above all it made it possible for me to enroll in Innsbruck University's doctoral program to round off my academics with economics and business law. Somehow I arranged my schedules between Germany, Italy and Switzerland so that the night trains would get me to my classes in time. My professors knew full well what I was doing, but they let me get away with my part-time studying because they were intrigued to have a German-American executive in their class rooms, especially in their seminars - a kind of symbiosis. They wanted to learn more about American business practices, especially in the then new field of 'Econometrics' which at Grace had become a brand new market research tool. As a result they made getting my doctorate easy by giving me 'Econometrics in Industry Applications' as my dissertation subject. It took me six years to get my doctorate.

Innsbruck is a beautiful city with old time Austrian charm, surrounded by the high Alps, world renowned for skiing and mountaineering - but not once, in all this time, did I find the time to do any of that.

Call it determination!

<O>

Working my Way through Europe

I was made Grace's European Technology Manager. It was hard work. Traveling around Europe in those days was not easy, with constant worries about visas, travel restrictions, hotel shortages and, above all, the looming Cold War with communist Russia. Personal safety was by no means guaranteed. And ever so often the managers of the local Grace offices were not entirely supportive of my work, viewing me as an intruder on their fiefdoms, and suspicious of my direct line to the big New York bosses. The powerful managers of the old time European chemical companies sometimes viewed Grace as a brash upstart. I had my hands full trying to make Grace their equal.

But there were also plenty of moments of triumph and even occasionally some level of hilarity.

At one point we had succeeded in selling licenses to several European petrochemical companies to produce the new High Density Polyethylene (the product of the Baton Rouge plant that I had helped start up a few years earlier). Teaching them how to produce it was one thing, but now they had to find markets for this new material - that, too, was my job. Together we looked high and low for applications in the automotive industries, in aircrafts, telephones and other promising markets, but it was slow going and their unsold plastics were piling up in their warehouses. I was on the spot. I had sold them the license and now they were 'breathing down my neck' for me to show them that I had not made empty promises. Then it happened that in the US, Grace had stumbled across a brand new market - the Hula Hoop toy that had swept the market requiring millions of pounds of this new material.

I was about to tell my European counterparts about it but suddenly had an idea: why give this new market away - let's make some extra money by asking for royalties! But how to go about it?

Making a bit of a mystery of this new application I asked my European licensees to sign a commitment letter to pay us royalties on all the plastics they would sell for this still undisclosed application. And - lo and behold - each of these powerful companies did sign my commitment letter, - so much trust I had built up in the years I had been working with them.

I asked them to meet me in our London office for the moment of disclosure. They all came, Sir Westnedge from Imperial Chemicals, Prof.Dr. Trieschman from giant BASF, Jean Daget from the French Petroleum Company, and Dr. Ricchardi from the Italian Solvay Group, complete with their retinue of technical and marketing staff. It was a formidable group that had gathered to hear from us about this great new application for their new plastic.

With Al Spaak, our manager of plastics technology in tow, I started to address these powerful European captains of industry by thanking them for their confidence. As they were leaning forward in their seats in anticipation of the great news I was about to tell them I pulled a sample of a hula hoop from behind the curtain and asked Al Spaak to demonstrate it to them. They sat there, speechless. How could Wolf Mack dare to come to them with a silly toy when they had expected some high-tech items that would be in keeping with their dignified positions! Had I overplayed my hand, was I about to lose the trust I had built up with them over years of hard work?

Then, one by one, they started to laugh, and with good reason: this silly American fad would take over Europe and they would empty their warehouses of the new material. Grace collected some nice royalties. It put me up another notch in their respect.

At another occasion Al Spaak and I were invited to a meeting at the sprawling Dutch States Mines chemical complex in Geleen in the South of Holland. To save us the long car ride from Schiphol airport they had sent their helicopter. When we arrived at the plant we were received by an honor guard, complete with military band and red carpet. More than slightly embarrassed we found out why: the flight manifest listed me and "Dr. Spaak" as passengers. They thought we had their Prime Minister on board, Dr. Henri Spaak (actually our Al Spaak's distant cousin). Well, everybody had a good laugh, but we had become famous in a funny way.

In the meantime, Grace's US plastics operations, too, were having a hard time finding markets for their plastic materials. In the search for applications of the new plastics the Europeans sometimes were ahead of us. I had noticed that in France gallon size plastic bottles were starting to appear in their grocery stores replacing the traditional glass milk bottles. I got hold of a few samples and traced them to a German company that had developed the way to make them - by a process called 'blow-molding', then an entirely new technology.

The US plastics division wanted me to help them with this new application. Armed with my sample we went to several New York based dairies - they were not interested: "Who would ever want to drink milk from a plastic bottle! And besides, our trade association would have to approve it first." We decided to take our case to the Washington DC based National Dairy Association - only cold shoulders.

Then, one of their aids took me aside. He had told some one from the office of the Senator from Tennessee of our efforts to introduce the plastic milk bottle, and that the Senator knew just the right people to get a plastic milk bottles project going - the money would be there. I made my proposal about the machinery to be procured and, sure enough, a check came with the order for me to proceed. The Senator's men would provide a suitable building in the middle of Tennessee's cattle country. Within a few months my new plant would churn out milk bottles by the thousands.

Funny thing - nowhere could we find milk sold in these bottles. When questioned about this, my man at the dairy association shrugged his shoulders.

Much later we found out that our new plastic bottles showed up with 'moon shine' inside - much handier than the clumsy old-fashioned stoneware jugs. The Senator from Tennessee did indeed know his people's real needs - and I learned from the pros that there are many ways for a savvy politician to get his votes.

Low and behold, before we knew it, the Tennessee dairies were following their moon-shine cousins' good example. They would be the first in the country to defy the glass bottle monopoly. Maybe the Senator had made a proposal they could not refuse..... And the Senator's plastics bottle plant thrived, expanded and they bought more and more machines - and our plastics. See: it does pay to 'know the right people'!

Back in New York the big boss, Peter Grace, stuck his head in my office, pointing his finger at me and said, in his notorious blunt ways that never would allow for any question or comment: "You are Catholic, right, and I am told you are good at plastics, and I want you to go to see my friend, Mrs.Daugherty in Dublin, and start making plastic rosaries." With that, he turned and left me pondering what this was all about. I knew that Peter's request was an order not to be questioned. Peter Grace, ardent Catholic, had gotten enamored with a movement headed by a Father Payton ("The family that prays together stays together"). He wanted rosaries, millions of them, to be distributed by the Missions in poor Latin American countries.

Well, off I was to Dublin to meet Mrs. Daugherty, the quintessential dowager right out of "Downton Abbey". She handed me the keys to an unused part of her chocolate factories and introduced an accountant with a seemingly unlimited checking account. She sent us a few dozen young Irish girls to do the work once I had procured the plastics molding machines and the molds, and soon we would turn out rosaries - thousands and thousands of them. All of a sudden I had become a shining example of how to put the new plastics into the service of Father Peyton's missions. I am not sure what benefits these poor natives of the Amazon jungles would drive from my plastic rosaries - certainly they had more pressing needs. No matter, it did not hurt my standing with Peter Grace and my career in his empire. I still have a few of those rosaries as a reminder of the many facets of my plastics 'pioneering' days. You just never know what surprises might be around the corner.....

Even as devout catholic Peter Grace did not shy away from employing former Nazi industrialist when it helped his ambitions to become accepted into the European industrial inner circles. To me some of these corporate 'consultants' were strange bed-fellows, indeed, but I had to work with them. There was Dr. Otto Ambros, former head of IG Farben's infamous 'Zyklon-B' poison gas production with its horrific use in Germany's death camps. Then there was Friedrich Flick, the steel magnate, who was sentenced as war criminal for having used slave labor for Germany's armaments production. Grace delegated me into Flick's Duesseldorf headquarters for several months to coordinate a futuristic-sounding project to transport liquified natural gas from Algeria's gas fields into northern European harbors. In the mid-1950s we were way ahead of the times and the project came to nothing. It is now a very important part of Europe's energy supply.

There was an interesting twist in my somewhat strained relations with these war criminals - a certain Hans Toelle had married my (distant) Rohrbach aunt Hedwig Eisenhut. He, too, had served time as a war criminal in the notorious Landsberg prison where he had become close friends with Ambros and Flick. In a curious twist of fate it gave me a strange type of 'in' with those criminals who treated me almost as 'family'. I did not like it. With all his show of devotion to catholicism Peter Grace saw nothing immoral in using war criminals when it helped him make even more money. I suspected that deep under there was probably some unsavory hidden sympathy with Naziism - and its insane anti-semitism.

No matter - I did enjoy my life between New York and the capitals of Europe. I had succeeded in making a name for myself in the hollowed halls of the European chemical giants. But I began to see that gradually my work had gotten me away from my original ambition to be the best engineer in my field as the demands of my work pushed me further and further into the task of managing projects, with other engineers assigned to me. I had to find out what managing really meant. As an engineer I was used to dealing with things, with materials, their strength, and how to apply them to construct buildings, machines or, in my case, plastics manufacturing plants.

As a manager I had to learn how to deal with people, how to direct their work, instead of doing the work myself. I had to learn how to monitor their effectiveness, all in the interest of maximizing monetary gains. But it was also about understanding what makes the professionals in my charge perform, to bring out the best of their abilities and to learn to navigate around their weaknesses. It meant to monitor their work habits and to know about their ambitions - like every one else, a professional will function well when he/she is paid attention to, and when their own personal goals are given a chance to unfold.

Like so many engineers who are pushed into managing positions I at first had some trouble with this new aspect of my work. With the usual 'one step forward, half a step back' type of learning I eventually had to master this transition from being a good engineer to being a manager - to develop the skill of causing the engineers in my charge to do the engineering work well, instead of me doing it myself, even when I thought that I could it much better, or faster. The obligatory course during my engineering studies, "The Psychology of the Work Place" finally paid off - I often wished I had paid more attention to this subject. Sometimes I even thought that most likely that course actually was the most important one in my entire engineering school curriculum!

All told, things looked good for me, my career blossoming, my bosses mostly happy with my work. I had become a part of the international engineering business community. I liked it, very much so.

Most important to me was freedom in scheduling my daily work. I would never want a 'Nine-to-Five' job in a rigidly controlled company with its inevitable politics of back-stabbing and claiming others' achievements for their own. And, finally, I wanted to get out from under the demoralizing status of 'wage slavery', of having to live from 'paycheck-to-paycheck'. I wanted very badly to become financially independent, at least to the point where I did not have to worry about my next paycheck. I was well on my way to getting there.

But deep under I knew something was missing, something of huge importance, to fulfill my life. And out of the blue came the answer. Literally, out of the sky.

<O>

Phases of our Lives

MARRIAGE

*"Marriage is the will of Two to create a One
which is more than those who created it".
(Friedrich Nietzsche, German philosopher, 1844-1900)*

Phases of our Lives

Francesca, Magical Francesca!

Accompanying two directors of the French company Pechiney on a flight to Grace's New York headquarter for yet another licensing negotiations I met this beautiful girl with the most delightful smile and the most soulful eyes. She was an Air Hostess with TWA on our flight to Newark. She moved ever so gracefully through all the turbulence, singing sentimental songs in her oh-so beautiful voice. Here is this fateful first dialogue with Francesca:

Me: "You must be happy to sing so nicely."

She: "No, not at all, I am so sad, I just broke an engagement."

Me: "Come and talk to me, *I'm a doctor.*"

Of course, that was a lie - I had not yet finished my dissertation, and certainly not in the medical field! But I somehow fantasized that she would become my love, my wife, my companion for life and the mother of my children. For that any little lie would be a good lie.

She did come to talk to me, dodging the frightening turbulence. Not content with this first sign of interest I decided to move further on: "Have you ever been to Europe?"

"No," she said but she actually had been planning a trip soon because she was about to transfer to TWA's prestigious international group and wanted to use some vacation time before her next assignment.

I forged ahead, knowing that I was taking risks that I might regret, but I said, "Would you like me to show you some of Europe?"

No sooner had I asked I kicked myself: "Dummkopf!" I said to myself, could I not think of something more intelligent to say? But I really meant it! She gave me this amused look, as if challenging me for a more trust-inspiring statement. Of course, I had one ready - I was indeed going to Europe on one of my routine trips, very soon . I gave her my business card: "I know you girls are busy, so why not call me when your are in town so that we can talk about Europe!"

Francesca thought that I must be married already. First of all, in America at that time men at my age (30!) were almost always married already, and me having given her my business card, not my home number, definitely raised a red flag. But then, when I left the plane, she noticed that I had a big hole in one of my socks. Would a wife let her man go on a business trip like that?

Francesca decided that all this was too strange and she would not call me (at my office!) for a long time. But then curiousity took over: she found me in the telephone book. I was living on Riverside Drive. She called my number a few times, during the day, just to see whether a woman would answer. Of course, there was no answer. But what if our cleaning women would have picked up the phone? Finally, after weeks, at her room mates prodding, Francesca called me at the office. "What took you so long!".

Our first date! We had cocktails in the (then) very fashionable Hotel Manhattan, went to see the "Marriage Go-around," followed by late dinner at Sardis', the famed hang-out for the New York theater crowd. She loved it, including my laughing the loudest at the play's witty lines.

My room mate Hans Furmans, savvy about travels in Europe, helped us map out Francesca's itinerary to overlap as much as possible with an upcoming business trip that would take me to Italy and France. The idea was for her to 'do' Rome and Venice, to meet Anneliese and her family in Luzern, and then we would rendezvous in Paris, once I would be finished attending the big Milan Plastics fair. And off she went on her first European adventure.

There was no hotel to be found for me in Milan, so I stayed in nearby Lugano, just across the border of Switzerland, an easy half hour commute from Milan. Tired from a long day at the Fair I trudged back to Milan's huge central train station to catch my commuter train to Lugano, dodging the usual Saturday evening crowds.

And then, out of nowhere I heard this familiar voice: "Here, Conrado, here with my baggage!" I could not believe it - here was my Francesca, trying to find her way - and her luggage - to the train to Lugano (her final destination being Lucerne). I tried to find her in the throngs of Italian commuters, saw her on the platform with Conrado and her baggage, went to embrace her, kissed her on both cheeks, took her luggage from a dumbfounded Conrado, shook his hand, thanked him for his help, and we just barely made it to the departing train.

Whew! What an unbelievable stroke of fate, but true! I knew of course that she was traveling in Europe, but she was scheduled to go through Milan on her way to my sister's a few days later. She had changed her mind, overwhelmed with a lot of unwanted attention showered on her in Rome and Venice by some over-eager Italians - something that could not have been surprising to the pretty blond American girl! She was on her way to meet my sister, a few days ahead of her original itinerary. Well, I said, why not come

with me to Lugano until it's time to go on to see Anneliese? By any standards of good behavior (it was, after all, still the 1950s!), that was not quite proper for me to ask - but she was thinking about it.

I took her to my quaint hill-side hotel, asking for a room for her, introducing her to the staid Swiss innkeepers as my friend from New York. The receptionist looked at us askance - no, there was no room here, but we could give you a room at our sister hotel ..... Off we went to find this very elegant hotel, with Francesca's suite overlooking gorgeous Lake Lugano. Wow again.

We had the most wonderful week-end, taking the regular lake boat, the funicular up Mount Salvatore, hiking for hours through the hills of the south Switzerland countryside, having a leisurely lunch at a mountain inn - and missing the last bus

back to town. We had to walk all the way back, for untold miles, dead tired but happy for being together. My respect for Francesca's ability to find joy in so many simple things, her good-natured dealing with the hardship caused by my lack of adequate planning showed me that there was so much more to her than I could possibly have known.

That day changed my life for good. Meeting in Paris (my next scheduled work week) sealed the deal. It was May Day, and I bought her the traditional little bouquet of May flowers

from the little girl on the corner. We went to the Eiffel Tower, then to Versailles where she went to buy a baguette, some sausage and cheese, and of course, the obligatory bottle of wine, and off we went

into the Versailles Castle gardens for a picnic on a lawn next to one of this place's famous fountains. Some American tourists passed us and we heard them say, "see, that is how the French do it!" We chuckled and celebrated a great day.

Francesca did everything in style - her European travels were picture-book studies in history, art and plain personal elegance. An excursion to the Jungfau? In great style. The fountains in Rome - like a movie star. But also don't forget to pet the Swiss mountain donkey! You have to know to enjoy life, people and places with all their diversity - a gift that few of us have,

Back in New York we would spend more and more time together. There were hikes in the snowy hills of the Bear Mountains, beach parties with her friends at their Westhampton seaside cottage,

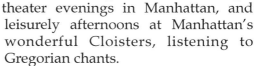

theater evenings in Manhattan, and leisurely afternoons at Manhattan's wonderful Cloisters, listening to Gregorian chants.

But the most exciting parts of our courtship were our meetings in Europe's capitals where we would somehow find ways to coordinate

Francesca's air line lay-overs with my schedules. I kept a car in several cities where Grace had offices (this was before the times of easy car rentals), a

silver convertible Porsche in Zurich, a white Mercedes SL sports car in Dusseldorf, and a red Jaguar in Paris. Meeting Francesca on her arrivals at the airports was always great fun - especially showing off to her oh-so-jealous colleagues. These were wonderful times together. Both us of were getting more serious about our relationship. - and also anxious what would be in store for us.

Of course, my trips to Europe were being planned less and less on the requirements of business and more about Francesca's flight schedule. I had fallen in love, deeply, and I knew what that would mean. Would it mean the same to Francesca?

I made the big decision. On a sunny early Spring day I invited her for an outing to our favorite Manhattan place - the Cloisters. We settled down in the great courtyard that had been lovingly reconstructed from the ruins of French monasteries in the 1930s under the WPA program. We sat there on the wall between the marble Romanesque columns and gazed at the Hudson River below us. In my inimitable ways I started to tell her about my life plans, that I wanted to have a close-knit family, play a role in the community, build a career by working together, cultivate good friendships - a life together, for good.

My speech became a bit long, but for me it was the way I wanted to make my 'proposal,' without the kneeling-down part. Perhaps Francesca expected a some more romantic proposal but for me the 'life plan' one was the overarching important part, much more in keeping with my deeper feelings.

To my happy surprise she said "YES," tears welling up in her beautiful eyes. This was also what she wanted in life - a closely knit family.

And above everything else - to be there for each other, unconditionally.

Always.

<O>

And so we got Married!

We were married in Manhattan's Santa Monica Church on August 29, 1962, celebrated with our New York friends in the "Top of the Sixes," with lunch at the glorious Four Seasons, and then off to Europe on our honeymoon, visiting my mother, sister and my relatives. None of them could be with us in New York - transatlantic travel was not quite as easy then as it is now. But when Francesca met Mama and all the rest of my German family they all embraced her warmly. Mama would be a good Mother-in-Law and Francesca always the most appreciative and patient daughter-in-law you could imagine - Mama happy that her only surviving son had found such a lovely and lovable girl to share his life.

Together, Francesca and I did all of what we had laid out for us in the days of our courtship. Together we would give real meaning to our lives, taking it to a totally different level. She would truly become my companion in life, supporting me in the ups and downs in business and follow me wherever we needed to go - to Germany, to Mexico, to New England, to our family place in New Jersey, our country homes and to our villa life in St. Barth, always making the family work together and finding so much joy in doing so. She would give us four great sons, and in due time they would form their own families and presented us with eleven fabulous grand children. Now, in our old age they are the joy of our lives.

And think of it: somehow, miraculously, that fateful flight from Columbus to Newark had changed everything. For that I will forever be grateful. It made everything worth while. All the changes I had seen in my life, the survival of a war, the long way through my education and my work life between New York and Europe finally made sense. And this time change came in a really big way, where it really mattered. Francesca gave it a new beginning altogether and the fulfillment of so many of our dreams. - the ultimate lesson of life.

<O>

What United Us

How do young people any place in this world get together for life? How does it happen that they meet in the first place? Is it that they see each other as complementing their own persona, or is it, as some would say, that opposites attract each other? Of course, all these are futile attempts to explain the un-explainable. The fact was, as millions before us, we just discovered that we were liking each other, and before we knew it, and with the right caring, the 'liking' became the 'loving'. That would override any thing else.

Yes, there were differences: Francesca forever the vivacious, spirited, the socially adept, the curious and the adventure-seeker, and then me, described by many friends and by others not so charitable, with a hand gesture indicating a 'square', bent on my studies, my career as an engineer and (eventually) a manager, and with my European ways - with my 'Queen's English' as I had learned it at school.

But after the difference you could see the striking similarities. In many ways we both did come from quite a comparable back ground - both our families had made themselves move from one level of cultural and socio-economic levels to another: after all, my father had been the first (and only) in his family to get some measure of higher education. My parents, too, were 'firsts' in the context of their times, having gone away form their ancestors' homes into a new world where they had to find their own place - in some ways they, too, were a sort of 'immigrant', albeit in their own country.

They certainly knew the difficulties of finding their place in a new environment.

And, like Francesca's family, we were a tightly knit bunch who had to learn the same values: stick together, help yourself and those in need, and try not to become a burden to any one else. Both of us had been raised in a family culture of orderliness, working together, from creating a warm family life, doing our daily chores, including the seemingly mundane habit of taking our meals together as a family. Even when it came to the English language, both of us learned it as a second language - Francesca after being raised first in Polish, and I, of course, in German. So, there was not much in our basic make-up that we had to 'adjust'.

It helped that we were brought up in the same religion, as Catholics, although we found out soon that my experiences as catholic were a bit different, the Church in Europe having gone through the fires of wars and political upheavals - and instead of insisting on narrow issues of doctrine it emphasized its humanistic social teachings. I found it kind of quaint that the American Catholics still would blindly believe in the many church dogmas that had elevated nice legends into hard doctrines that would decide whether you would be going to heaven or not. Blind faith was driven out of us Europeans by the stark realization that the Church as an organization had lost its credibility as a result of its utter failure to its flock by its complicity with the Nazis.

Historically, the Church had almost always sided with the earthly powers - always ready to sacrifice the well-being of their flock to their own needs for job security. That was certainly the case in Nazi Germany. It would take the American Catholics another few generations to discover the sad truth of the Church's shortcomings, precipitated by its clergy's sexual transgressions. We understood quite well that the Church as an earthly organization was populated with people like us and therefore not immune to sin. So, we just had to learn to separate the organization from its wonderful teachings.

But to us, those were not issues that would divide us. We were happy that we had enough similarities in up-bringing and in our basic sets of values. We could go right ahead with the task of building our own family - on the foundations and the example of those that had been before us. And to do it the way we had vowed to each other: to be there for each other at all times, to build a close relationship among the two of us, and be attentive to the needs of our children. We both very strongly believe that once we have committed to each other we absolutely must support each other.

Not to 'be there for each other in all circumstances', to go one's own way at the expense of the other, is a horrible sin, a fundamental lack of basic human decency. Not to be there for one's children, to ignore them when they are asking for their mother's (or their father's) attention is a crime against their natural development. Children that are ignored will be vulnerable to lack of self-respect, and will be prone to tantrums as their only way to get the attention they crave. Parenting is a responsibility that must be shared, and embraced, by both parents, no matter what. Failure to so is a form of disloyalty and betrayal, just as damaging to a relationship as sexual infidelity.

Too often we had seen others making these mistakes, and we vowed not ever to fail each other in these basic obligations, basic to every human relationship.

Phases of our Lives

My Pennsylvania-Polish Connection

At first sight it might have appeared to outsiders that we had come from different back grounds - Francesca from the quintessential Polish immigration family, me fresh from Germany from a typical middle level civil service family. We found out soon that there were many more similarities in our upbringing than what might appear. Francesca's grandparents had come to Pennsylvania, worked hard, their American born second generation working themselves out of the coal mines into better jobs, build their nice clapboard homes on the tree lined streets of their chosen town of West Wyoming. They were active in their church, helped each other grow, continued in the vein of the time- honored values of the 'old country' but also embracing the 'American way', seeking to better themselves - I have never met any one who was as voracious a reader as my future father-in-law "Matty". Always ready to tell a good story he would be following politics, local and national, and go hunting and fishing with his sons. His political discussions with his friends, Walter Huntz and future in-law Joe Solomon were legendary, and often quite passionate. They were very much into

politics and they knew a lot about it. And in Pennsylvania there was indeed a lot going on, always.

Matty did photography, in his days still a somewhat new and exotic hobby, developing his own films in a basement closet equipped with the trays for the developing and the 'fixation' solutions. The family pictures shown here are all his creation.

I loved it when he would take me on long car rides showing me his beloved Pennsylvania, especially the farm lands to the north along the beautiful Susquehanna river. He very much wanted to buy one of the farms in the rolling hills near the New York state line. Nothing came of this idea, much to his (and my) regret.

Francesca's mother, "Annie" would keep the family together with good teachings, superb cooking and ever-ready good advice - whether sought or not. You would never hear her speak unkindly about any one. They lived good all-round lives. They saw to it that all their children, the third generation, would become good Americans, would attend college, become dentists, home economics teachers and find good jobs. But their values, their moral standards, continued like the 'old country' way - good work ethics, taking care of their own needs, but ready at any time to help others who needed help - exactly the same values that were taught in my German family. They all had worked hard and became modestly prosperous, they owned their homes, they made a good living. Some owned grocery stores, some were into building homes, one started a dairy. They were aspiring middle-class people, living modestly but enjoying a good measure of economic security.

I would get to know Francesca's Pennsylvania family as my very warm and welcoming in-laws, even to me having come from Germany, historically not the Poles greatest friend, and certainly not during the times when the Greskiewiczes and the Klockos had come to America. I tried, of course, to put my best foot forward, sometimes perhaps a bit too eager to find their acceptance, sometimes not very smartly. One time, at one of their great family dinners, I started into the Polish-German history. Francesca's maternal grandparents had come from Krakow, the historic capital of Poland. Turning to her father, he told me that his family had come from Poznan. OK, when? About 1870some. Well, I said, then you are actually German because Poznan (Posen) at that time had been part of Germany..........Wow. Need any more proof of my great diplomatic skills? It had gotten very still around the table. Francesca probably would have kicked me under the table had I been within reach. It took a while for them to overcome the shock of my gross insensitivity, but they did and I would eventually become one of them, truly.

Polish people had immigrated to the US from many different backgrounds. Some, for sure, had come here in the hope to lifting themselves out of poverty. However, quite a few came here for totally different reasons. In the 1800s Poland had seen a growing oppression by Russia to their East and aggressive land grabs by Germany from the West, both competing with each other for Poland's resources. Both were conscripting young Poles into their armies and many young Poles fled their country to avoid this much dreaded fate. Then both the Germans and the Russians began to force Polish landowners from their properties to incorporate them in their own estates. Francesca's grandfather Ignatius kept telling about the place where he had grown up, describing "a large self-contained walled farm estate with land as far as you could see. The many people who worked on the farm lived behind the walls and the gates were locked at night. The fireplace, so big a man could stand up in it and several could sleep on its mantle...."

Not much was made of his story until much later when Francesca was an air hostess with TWA. One day she had two Polish passengers on board - she heard them speak in Polish to each other. When she made her routine flight announcement ("I am Francesca Greskiewicz, your hostesss on this flight.....") these two passengers came running to her: "Are you Miss Greskiewicz? Do you know Ignatius Greskiewicz?" "Of course, he was my grandfather!" "Where can we find him?" Well, he had been dead by then many years. How would these two Polish men know of her grandfather Ignatius? When they debarked they kissed her hand, in good traditional Polish fashion but left without contact information. What was this all about? Grandpa Matty shrugged it off: "These men were probably from the Polish government looking to collect back-taxes on the land or something like that." Remember: these were the years when a lot of reclaiming of properties in East Europe took place. Very curious indeed. Perhaps Grandfather Ignatius' stories were true after all? Perhaps Francesca was even a Polish princess? She certainly had all the attributes - pretty, vivacious and very bright!

You can see that even as a little girl she was looking out, eyes

wide open for the unknown. She was the one with the adventurous spirit, wanting to see the world, certainly the world beyond their beloved Wyoming Valley. Look at her as the little girl, Dad's apple of the eye: looking out, ready to venture.

Look at her with her cousins - the leader of the pack, and certainly the prettiest. Look at her, the cheerleader: exuberance personified.

She excelled at school but the pull of adventure took over. She wanted to become an air hostess, at that time a very coveted and prestigious job that only very few young girls would meet the prerequisites: they not only had to be attractive but would be tested thoroughly for social graces, nursing abilities (for emergencies) and physical stamina - airplane travel at that time (the 1950s) was so much different, demanding much better skills and social abilities than now - after all, airplane passengers were the 'upper crust' and the services offered were accordingly 'first class'. Francesca made it - the only one among 250 applicants. After two years of flying 'domestic' she was invited to join the elite international crews, for the coveted European routes. She made the best of it, spending her long lay-overs in Paris, Rome, Frankfurt, London, Madrid and Lisbon, seeing their historic sites, visiting their art galleries and taking in their cultural lives.

These days of the Cold War brought also much anxiety about the safety of Europe - and the Americans traveling there. Francesca would see streams of refugees, some from Eastern Europe where - surprise - her Polish language knowledge came in very handy.

She also saw history being made. She happened to be in Germany when, on August 13 of 1961 the infamous 'Berlin Wall' came up to divide Berlin in an East and a West part. Some 28 years later, when this wall finally came down, Francesca and I happened to be in Germany, again, in Cologne, to see the stunned West Germans wondering how they would cope with this new reality. It was not the euphoric celebration that the world expected. The West Germans knew that it would take many years and untold billions of Marks to get the East Germans back into the Western fold, having been changed so much during two generations of communist brainwashing.

Kind, gentle mother Annie died of Addison's disease much too early, at age 63. With proper medical knowledge her untimely death could have easily been avoided - medical care was not what it should have been. 'Grandpa' Matty would live to a ripe age of 86, surrounded by his family that in his time had grown to include eleven grandchildren.

We both wanted to develop an ever closer relationship with Francesca's Pennsylvania family. Francesca organized many, many family get-togethers in our home, with fabulous meals, indoors and on our decks, or on the lake. It gave me an excellent opportunity to get to know her family, as she would get to know those of my family who visited us.

It was fascinating to see how each of Francesca's siblings pursued different aims and developed their own way of living. One thing they all had in common was Grandpa Mathews' unquenchable thirst for reading, for self-improvement. His five children and his grand-children did what the 'American Dream' is all about - they learned and became successful, each in different ways. And different they all were: it has always astounded me how sons and daughters of the same family, with the same genes and up-bringing, can turn out to so different from each other, in temperament, ambition and interests. This certainly was true in my family, with brothers Hermann and Waldemar being so different, and sister Anneliese again with very different outlooks on life. And, of course, it was very much so in Francesca's family.

Francesca's older sister Tess, forever the calm, collected care-giver, and sometimes lovingly referred to as the 'family matriarch', married Joseph Solomon, a teacher, who would become my friend, perhaps the best I ever had. She joined Penn State University's Outreach Program to teach new-comers to this country better ways to establish their hou. holds in their new environments and to create more nutritious meals for their families. Her association with Penn State helped all four of her children get their undergraduate degrees there. Her oldest son Jimmy went on to become an eminent maxillofacial surgeon, son John a food technologist, son Joe a university administrator, and daughter Joan became an Industrial Engineer (I know first hand how much work had to go into that!). With great pride she is looking at her six grandchildren, bright, ambitious, all of them. How else can you define a family's success?

Francesca's older brother Len, always outgoing and gregarious, liked to be with his friends and with former schoolmates. Ebullient, funny and also sometimes irascible, Len married Anne, right back from his tour of duty in Korea. In rapid sequence they had three  children: Annie, Mark and Richard. Anne battled cancer for six long years after her last pregnancy, making the arrival of her baby into

this world with great difficulties. And then disaster struck: five year old Mark died in a terrible car accident, and Len was on the brink himself, for weeks in intensive care. It was a very difficult time for Len. During Ann's very long and agonizing sickness, toddler Annie and infant Richard were cared for by his wife's mother. Len's job required him to be away from home a lot, making it difficult for him to spend much time with his children.

After his wife's death, his parents stepped in to take care of Annie and Richard, with sister Florence giving a hand. At that time Len's older sister Tess and her husband Joe also lived there with their own three toddlers until they had found a place of their own. They, too, helped care for Len's children.

When Len married Judy, Francesca did the wedding in her gracious style. Judy had two children of her own from her previous marriage but became a mother also to Len's children. After graduating from Penn State, Annie went on her own, working for Disney in New York and on the West Coast. Richard moved in with Len's younger sister Florence in New Jersey during his young adult years. During all these years, Len continued in his traveling job, not being able to spend much time with his family.

Annie and Richard would spend many summer months in our home growing up with our sons. Francesca became like a mother to the two while they were motherless for many years. Annie still remembers fondly those bonding times in our family. Richard, now in his fifties, is in his own world, living in New Jersey.

Len had gone to Kings, a small and very Catholic local college. He turned out to be a shrewd investor. As one of the very early UPS employees, he took full advantage of the company's very generous investment plans. He worked hard, with very long hours. Len took just about all his earnings to invest in UPS stock and they matched his investments, and eventually he got very wealthy and became one of the Company's top share holders.

Len does have a very generous vein - we always appreciated his hospitality in his great Florida condos, in his rambling Shavertown home and, of course, in his grand lakeside log house. He still likes very much to be with his friends, most from his UPS days, when Len was able to help them getting jobs which made them prosperous as well. And above all, Len generously supports the Church were he sought, and probably found, consolation for all the heartache of the loss of his son Mark, his first wife Anne's long-time sickness, and the times when the demands of his job prevented him from spending more time with his children while they were in their formative years.

For Francesca family means everything. Forever nurturing, she is always ready to take on her nieces and her nephews, my European relatives, and, of course, our own sons' numerous friends. From our early Wyckoff days so many of our friends still remember fondly her annual Easter egg hunt for  dozens of neighborhood children - people were anxiously anticipating being invited to this fun event. She created great homes for us and wanted to share what we had with her larger family, with untold family get-togethers, great meals, fun in our yard, our pool and the lake, and skating in New Jersey's often brutally cold winters.

We both wanted to do our best to help her younger brother Ed and her 'little' sister Florence in their attempts to find a place in this competitive world.

Like his big brother Len, Ed had gone to Kings College, and he wanted to become a doctor. Francesca and I supported him at medical school in Philadelphia as much as we could. It was not easy for us. I had started a new job and made only a modest salary. To broaden his world views we sent him on a European tour during which he was out of communication for quite a while. We were worried until he surprised us by showing up in Switzerland just as we were visiting Anneliese's family in Lucerne - quite to our relief.

Two years into med school he decided to switch to dentistry. He would build up a successful practice, first in nearby Honesdale, PA, and then in the pretty New England college town of Williamstown. A bachelor, he took early retirement in the Montana mountains, becoming an accomplished big game hunter and fly fisherman.

'Little sister' Florence went to Wilkes College and studied journalism. To help her in her transition from school to the work place we organized a trip to Europe on a student ship after graduation to broaden her views on this world and to visit Anneliese and my Mother. She liked Gengenbach so much that she did not want to come back. We finally had to put our foot down as our own finances had been stretched to a point where we had difficulties ourselves to make ends meet. Back in the USA she got a job in New York city with Saturday Evening Post.

Not content with the every day grind of journalism she wanted to follow Francesca's steps and became an air hostess with PanAm. Florence was a PanAm hostess for almost 20 years. Francesca made a beautiful wedding reception for her at our Wyckoff home. When she lived in Tokyo she used our Franklin Lakes home as her base, commuting between JFK and her home in Tokyo.

Once she had moved back to the US, we were happy to help her and her darling little Whitney with her home in charming Roseland. Unfortunately her marriage would end. Through hard work and determination, little Whitney would become a renowned horse veterinarian and is now practicing in nearby Poulsbo in the beautiful Northwest, less than one hour away from us. She is working hard to pay off her sizable student loans.

Both Francesca and I have always taken pride that we would pay for the best education that our our sons could get. It was not that we always had plenty of money, but we lived simply, and just did not spend money on luxuries. We chose to spend our money on our sons' education and on useful apprenticeships, here and abroad, to enlarge their world views. Never would we want to send our sons into their adult lives with any form of debt hanging over their heads.

Those of us who are concerned about our mounting national debt should be very critical of our very bad habit of letting our sons and daughters be penalized by our unwillingness to face up to the very basic fact that higher education is of fundamental importance to our nation and needs to be properly funded. Financing this basic need via 'student loans' is fiscally irresponsible - it is a case of 'kicking the can down the road' of the worst kind.

For our economy, it is an unmitigated disaster - it has added over a trillion dollars to our nation's indebtedness. How did we get into this deplorable situation? It is largely the result of our financial institutions using their 'influence' to make our legislators do their bidding. The banks collect obscene interest from our hapless students and on top they get subsidies from us taxpayers, laughing all the way - 'to the bank'.

By the same principles Francesca and I declined all scholarship offers that our sons received for their achievements in academics or sports. We always believed that this type of financial aid should be only for those whose parents truly could not pay for their education. We were not about to take the financial aid for educational opportunities away from the poor.

Maybe we just have a different view of parents' obligations to their off-springs - we believe that we ourselves should use our own resources in supporting their efforts to form the basis of their future lives.

<O>

Phases ofour Lives

WORKING TOGETHER

Phases of our Lives

And so our Married Life began

    Francesca and I were determined to live our lives together in all its aspects. Our motto: "Always be there for each other".

    To build a family was first. But we also wanted to be partners in all outside activities, in our social life, in our involvements with the community - and in my work, in my career.

    The first test of our lofty expectations came quite unexpectedly. 'Right off the bat' my job with W.R.Grace was the first to throw us into turmoil. No sooner we were married, Grace decided to move its European Division to Cambridge, Mass. It was done for no other reason than to accommodate its top management - most of them New England 'Blue Bloods'. But it suited us just fine - we were thrilled to be given an opportunity to live in the Boston area! Francesca quickly found a great apartment - the top floor of an old rambling house near Harvard Square, a few minutes from my new office. Life in New England was good - a new world had opened for us.

    In the middle of Boston's legendary winter our first son was born - Wolfgang Adam Jr, a bit early, but healthy and eager to get to know us and his new world. We had become a real family. Francesca became the proverbial doting mother, and I learned, slowly but surely, to be a

father. With all of that, we learned to find a new balance between the novelty of being a parent, the life in our new surroundings and the demands of my work which still would take me to Europe every other month. It was certainly not easy for Francesca, far from the support structure of her family, and with guys like the ominous 'Boston Strangler' lurking everywhere. But Francesca was brave and unquestioningly supportive of the many demands of my job.

In the meantime, more and more of the focus of my duties in Europe had shifted from London to the Paris office. This suited me just fine - I liked being in France, my fluency in French helped, and so did the proximity to my hometown and to my Mother. The French managers wanted me to join them as their technical VP. Even though my salary would be lower, in line with French standards, the offer was very attractive and would come with the coveted VP title. They told me to look for an apartment - I found a great little place on Parc Montsouris. Could not wait to tell Francesca the news - she loved the idea to move to Paris.

It was not to be.

Mexico - exciting Mexico

Back in Cambridge I found a note to see Walt Robbins, Peter Grace's right hand man in New York. His news: yes, I was wanted by the French group, but Grace had a more pressing need for me in Mexico............*Mexico*? What did I know about Mexico? I hardly spoke Spanish at that time. Why me?

As it turned out the Mexican offer was even better than the French offer. I would be 'Number Two' man, in charge of all technical matters, under Jorge Lopez, scion of a leading Mexican family. He was married to 'BJ', as we would get to know her, a lady from Texas who, as we would discover, was one of Mexico City's leading hostesses. And my ssalary would be in the almighty US Dollar! An offer I could not possibly refuse. So I moved back to New York to join Grace's Latin American Group.

We found a great apartment in Peter Cooper Village, almost in walking distance to my office at Hanover Square. It was a great city place for our little son Woefle, then a year and a half - and for Francesca to pursue her art classes. I started to commute to Mexico City to begin with my assignment - to consolidate six newly acquired chemical and plastics operations into one big new plant in Toluca, an hour west of the city. I found the land to build on, got the permits, hired a team of first class Mexican engineers, planned the operations, specified the equipment and so on. After one year of commuting, Grace decided to move me to Mexico City with our family.

In the meantime we were blessed with the arrival of son Christoph Eduard (named after my father). Not even three months old, he would become a resident of Mexico - his first words to be Spanish : "Calle, calle!".

Nothing, of course, is ever simple. Literally the day before we were to leave for our new place in the Grace empire a letter came from Germany - from a company with the unlikely name of 'Werner & Pfleiderer' offering me the job of President of their newly established US company, located in northern New Jersey.

This offer had not come entirely out of nowhere. As a part of my duties as manager of Grace's European business I had been commissioned with showing the directors of that German group Grace's new polyethylene plant in Baton Rouge. I did so, a year or so earlier, and obviously must have made quite an impression on Guenther Fahr, Managing Director of the powerful WP group of companies. Dr Fahr had offered me the President's job based on that encounter. I would also become a partner in WP's American venture. A part owner, and a shareholder!

What to do? Francesca agreed with me that the Mexican job was the real thing, and we would tell Fahr so.

We thoroughly enjoyed our life in Mexico. We took in the country's great history, the sophistication of its upper class and the unique cultural attractions. Francesca became a most sought after tour guide for our visiting friends and the many New York executives and their wives who came for a respite from winter (under the usual pretext of having to check up on their thriving Mexican Division). She would join her friend BJ in throwing incredible parties, mostly meant to hold our diverse employees together by giving them a sense of a larger family.

Surely we lived the life of 'rich gringos', and Francesca very quickly mastered the intricate tasks of the 'Señora', ruling over half a dozen staff and a grand house in the heart of fashionable Lomas de Chapultepec. We learned to speak Spanish and we tried to do justice to our host country's rich history and its customs. Amazing how little we Americans know about our neighbors to the South - Mexico

is a lot more than the poor workers that harvest our foods and build our homes.

We kept as close to the real Mexico as we could, shopping in the City's great Merced, and roaming the great Mexican country side. We were lucky, experiencing the best period in Mexico, its glorious 'Golden Era' (the mid-1960s). Francesca had the skill, the tact and the charm to make us most welcome everywhere.

For me it was hard work - typically ten hours a day, often Saturdays. I was determined to accomplish my task in record time,  and thankfully I had a superb team to help me. Within one year my new plant was up and running. Counting the first year working at it from New York it took just two years from inception to completion - even today a very unlikely schedule. I just wanted to make a name for myself as a capable project manager. I succeeded so well that Grace told me to go to Columbia to take over the same consolidation work there. Well, I had no intention to be thrown from one job in Latin America to another. It showed me that corporate America, revered so much at that time, had its not so benevolent side - it had little respect for the interests of their employees and the well-being of their families. I wanted  stability for my family, a place were we could grow roots.

Until then, my main interest had been to prove myself in the world of plastics technology, to hone my ability to make important contacts and to make them useful for my employer,

the Grace Group of companies. But now my goals were changing - I now had a young and growing family, and the interests of the family became more important.

Mexico was a great place to achieve all of this - it had culture, sophistication, a colorful every day life. I could not see any of that for my family in South America's hinterlands.

All of a sudden, the German WP offer looked a lot better to us. I accepted.

Leaving Mexico was not so easy. We had been thrown into an entirely new set of circumstance, far from any of our families' support structures, in a new country with a language we had to learn, and together we conquered it. We showed to each other that we were indeed there for each other, that we could rely on each other, no matter what, just as we had vowed to each other going into our marriage. We now knew for sure that on top of loving each other we also were becoming true partners in all our endeavors. We were a couple, in unison facing whatever we needed to do to to deal with life's uncertainties.

We had made life long friends. Two of them threw elaborate 'despedida' parties - in grand Mexican style, bull fights included. I was offered the ultimate tribute - I was to do the fighting of the bull. Well, it was a rather small one, but believe me, when you stand alone facing this animal in the bull rink it looked awfully big to me......

So, with tears and a bit of a heavy heart, we left Mexico.

<O>

My German Connection

I had known the German Werner Pfleiderer Group as a powerful and greatly respected industrial giant at the forefront of modern processing technology. First came a six months stay in the Stuttgart main plant 'to learn the business'. I delved into this task, determined to quickly become an expert in WP's technology, and to develop the relationship with its key people so that I would have their support in my coming work with them. Not an easy task considering their very ingrown structure.

It was certainly not easy for Francesca. WP had procured for us an apartment in the middle-class suburb of Bad Cannstadt, twenty minutes from the main WP manufacturing plant. By the German standards of the sixties the apartment was adequate, but after our glamourous life in Mexico it was quite a let-down, to say the least. The dark winter days could lead anyone to despair, and the neighbors were not friendly at all. Unlike in Mexico, there was no company-based social life in Stuttgart. Not once did we get a social invitation from the company's brass. At first we felt snubbed, but this is how the Germans did it at that time. I would leave before daybreak and return often after dark, trying to cram as much as possible into the available 'learning the business' schedule.

The good thing was that we were able to visit with my relatives and friends from school. Francesca loved picturesque Gengenbach and Rohrbach (still very much the farming town then). Her favorite

Rohrbach family: Onkel Heinrich, forever witty with his down-to-earth farmer's wisdom, and kind aunt Emilie. Their grandchildren Michaela, Ilona and Alexandra later on would spend long summers with us in Franklin Lakes.

Then we found out that Francesca was pregnant with our third son, to be named Eric Mathew, after Francesca's dad. Francesca was brave, coping with a not so friendly German environment and my very long hours. It was good that my mother would come for weeks on end to keep Francesca company, and the two bonded so well.

In those trying days I had to ask myself often "what have I done", having left the prestigious Grace company and a wonderful life in Mexico? But I was not about to give up, although I could very well have returned to my Grace career, what ever the conditions of a re-entry might be there. I had to remind myself that one of the reasons for having taken the WP offer was that it would afford me the opportunity to run my own show - the WP Board had given me this assurance.

I knew already that the fledgling US WP company was in bad shape - this was why they took me, an outsider, to turn things around. They had tried to apply their German set of circumstance to their little US subsidiary, making every decision by the Stuttgart headquarters. Also, WP was simply not known in America. The Germans made the simplistic assumption that just because theirs was a 'household name' in European industrial circles that they should have easy sailing here. They had no idea how much the managers of the American industries mistrusted foreign equipment that would potentially expose them to the uncertainties of service and technical support from abroad.

My first objective was to overcome the perception of questionable reliability as a foreign entity. Almost all of the twelve (!) original employees were transplants from the German WP company, and few had even tried to assimilate, which did nothing to overcome the hesitations by potential customers here to buy 'foreign'. We had to become an American company.

The first action was to change the company's name from the almost unpronounceable "Werner&Pfleiderer" to the simple "WP Corporation" (WPC for short), eventually to become our brand, so to speak. We added a number of very capable American engineers as well as carefully selected people from WP Stuttgart. As a matter of common courtesy I asked the Germans only to speak English, especially when non-English speakers were in earshot. The German company was run on traditional authoritative principles - by contrast, I encouraged individual initiative and participation in decision making - even to make a mistake was ok, but not to make it twice.

I wanted them to look at WPC as place where they could unfold their abilities and to become true professionals, to be respected by their peers and by their customers. We supported every one's active participation in engineering societies, and I, too, became a 'regular' giving presentation to regional and national groups. I liked very much the increasing invitations as guest lecturer at our leading engineering schools. Rubbing shoulders with their faculty gave me an opportunity to influence their engineering and science curriculum to give their students a better chance of landing good jobs after graduation.

Francesca made it a point to draw their wives into the "WPC Family", and we would include them in our regular management meetings, at Francesca's initiative, increasingly conducted at America's best resorts. It was meant to weld all of us together for the common interest of giving everyone at WPC an opportunity for a first class career, all while getting WP established as the dominating factor in our specialty technology, called compounding, blending different plastics and incorporating pigments and reinforcing agents, to satisfy the growing need for better plastics parts. Today's electronics, medical devices or airplanes cannot do without them.

The German WP had a very hard time swallowing this 'Americanization of WPC'. On top of that, after analyzing their different product lines I decided to use all my available resources on only one of them - their twin-screw compounding extruders. This was the only line that was innovative, with a substantial technology content, and therefore with a good niche potential for the US market. Their other product lines were 'low-tech' with very limited profit potential and fast growing competion from low-cost producers. Hanging on to there 'traditional' product lines actually weakened the German WP Group and would contribute substantially to its eventual demise. Of course, my decisions did not please the German managers of these older lines - they all wanted the glory of a US presence.

Throughout my tenure with WPC they were a thorn in my side as they would constantly try to 'steal' my hard won resources to promote their product lines in America, even though they could not generate profits. I was able to fend them off only because with my focussed approach, the extruder line became hugely successful - after a few years of hard work, WPC had grown to very respectable size. Most gratifying for me was that the WPC team had become much sought-after in our industry for their expertise and their reputation for professionalism and ethical dealings. This, above all, was the best legacy I could generate for them - and for myself.

I ran WPC for almost twenty years, building the best technical team in the industry. Together we made the company grow in size, profitability and the respect we earned by our customers.

In order to make WPC truly an American company I was determined to evolve from being just an importer of German made machinery into a full-fledged US based manufacturing company. With this new business model we started first to produce the essential spare parts and then, gradually, entire compounding machines. We succeeded beyong expectations. Our American customers loved it.

But even at that, the North American market for our particular lines of plastics processing equipment was only that big, and while it was growing at an above average rate, I wanted to make WPC into a much bigger factor on our markets. I saw that our customers (even very large companies like Du Pont, GE, Union Carbide) were asking us for more and more engineering services for the installation of our equipment and its integration into their manufacturing systems. They had, of course, their own engineering staff, but it was inefficient for them to learn all about our equipment and the entire production system evey time they would buy an extruder fom us. So, we started to offer complete engineering and design services along with our pieces of equipment. We were becoming an engineering company, much more than just an equipment supplier. Acquring a very early 1978 version of computers (the "Intergraph" system) gave us a leg up in systems design, much to the envy of the German parent company that was agonizingly slow in adopting these 'new-fangled' ways.

This broadening of our scope of supply got us involved with one of WPC's first opportunities with a global business concept. What happened was that our US customer Chevron had made a huge investment in a Saudi Arabia petrochemical complex for which they wanted to buy big WP extruders. Saudi Arabia was, of course, not at all our territory, but Chevron was our US customer, and on top, they had commissioned a US engineering company with procuring all the equipment.

I proposed to the German WP Board that WPC, not the German WP company, would become the seller of these big pieces of equipment. They were furious with me for even suggesting such an 'invasion into their territory' as they saw it. They certainly did not want us (and me personally) to make big money from this huge project. But I honestly could not see how the Germans could deal effectively with the American Chevron and their US based engineering company.

Our customer Chevron helped to break the deadlock by simply insisting on dealing only with a US based company. Furthermore they wanted to be offered not only the main pieces of machinery but also the entire engineering package for installation and the start-up services. We, at WPC, could perform under this request, but the German WP could not. We got the order, with several big ones to follow over the years.

Needless to say, my German counterparts did not like this a damn bit, and for the rest of my tenure with the WP group they would not let me forget that I had mortally wounded their pride. But for our WPC team a big new world had opened up. The WPC team was thrilled to be able to deal internationally and to travel to far away countries, first, of course, to Saudi Arabia, then to Japan, China and India. It greatly enlarged their horizons and did wonders for their chances to advance, with WPC and, if they would choose so, with other international engineering companies. And for me it was the beginning of my doing business in many places on this Earth with the technologies I had developed.

During my last five years with the WP Group the German parent company began to change. As competition in their old-time product lines stiffened they refused to let go of these venerated relics of 'the good old days' when they had dominated these markets. As a result they got into financial trouble. In order to prop up their dwindling cash position they started to drain the resources of their American holdings. I did not like that a bit as it was eating into the value of my own shareholdings. Eventually WP Germany had to be sold to a European financial group and this spelled the end to my managerial freedom. After almost twenty years of a good place in the German-American orbit it was time for me to look elsewhere for my future business activities.

This is when I decided to go off on my own. I became an entrepreneur. And so did Francesca.

<O>

Me and Francesca: the Entrepreneurs

It did not take long for me to find my place in this new atmosphere of being on my own. I had accumulated a good amount of capital, and I had already several new businesses in my sights. And after our sons had left our home to build their own lives, Francesca was ready to join me in my new endeavors.

We formed Mack Engineering Corp. and built several small plastics

compounding plants in Mexico, Taiwan, and especially India, where my friend Assis Bannerji introduced me to a group of Indian industrialists (the Bannerjis are still among our best friends). Francesca would travel with me to these exotic places which at that time were not anywhere as accessible as they are now (this was in the late 1980s!). I could have continued in these lucrative markets, even though it meant incessant traveling, but new opportunities came up in the US.

I became interested in developing new technologies for plastics recycling. In my earlier work I had done much to help the plastics industry grow, but I had become very much aware also of the mounting problem of the plastic waste stream. After all, most plastics were meant to eventually be thrown away. The landfills were overflowing with plastic waste. I was convinced that something needed to be done to deal with it.

This was 1986, and doing something like recycling of plastics was

not on too many people's minds. Plastics were cheap, and so much new plastic materials were being produced that the idea of re-using them did not make the plastics producers very happy. But there were enough voices outside of industry that wanted something done to cope with the ever increasing waste problem. I decided to make a business out of this new idea of finding second uses for plastics.

Francesca joined me in forming Polymerix Corp. to organize the collection of plastics waste and to convert it into 'plastic lumber', a most likely product for a large scale re-use of waste plastics. We took Polymerix Corp. public (NASDQ) and raised enough money to built a large plant on Long Island to extrude our patented glass fiber reinforced 'TriMax'. It found ready markets, from park benches all the way to sea walls. We were going strong.

TRIMAX®

But it became clear that in order to continue to grow we had to 'go national'. Along came US Plastic Lumber Inc. who had already become nation-wide. We merged Polymerix into this much bigger firm and cashed out.

There was a problem with using mixed plastic waste. In order to make good plastic lumber we had to wash the waste plastic to remove much of the the dirt, residual food and labels that always come with any plastic recycling scheme. Washing in itself was not the problem but we had to somehow clean up this wash water - no way could we dump it into the local sewers. So, together with my friend and business partner Al Moellenbeck, we developed a novel wastewater treatment system - digesting the organic portion of the waste water with targeting microbes. At that time this was a totally new technology, and again we were way ahead of the times. We formed BioTech Industries Inc. and started to market our system nation-wide. Francesca joined us as Marketing Director, and son Eric, fresh from

graduating in Environmental Sciences (!) became our chief technician, his first job after college.

'Manning' our booth at the very large Washington D.C. Environmental Conference Francesca even made the connection with the British company Simon Engineering which eventually bought BioTech. We made good money, and Eric went with Simon's California unit as their BioTech specialist. It turned out to be a somewhat difficult job for him but he obviously learned a lot about corporate life. I am sure it helped him to deal with the complexities of his later career.

Did it feel good to be your own boss? You bet it did. All that counted was success with our customers. No more company politics, no more back stabbing, robbing other's achievements. It was also an awful lot of work.

Our foray into the world of entrepreneurship had payed off well. It gave us the wherewithal for the travels to come and for our wonderful 'homes away from home'.

And I could now afford to follow the calls to serve on a number of Boards of industrial companies and college. Almost inevitably I had become a part of the industrial establishment. The powerful national Society of Plastics Industries (SPI) and the Society of Plastics Engineers (SPE) invited me into their Boards. Their quarterly meetings typically were held at America's best resorts, and Francesca took great delight in scouting sites, preparing the meetings and their glamourous social events. She became a leader every bit as much as I.

In my position as SPI Treasurer I got quite a glimpse at the workings of lobbyists, at the federal and state levels. Whatever illusions I might have held as to the lofty conception of our government agencies evaporated quite quickly when I saw SPI's big public relations group in action. As Treasurer I had to create and supervise the PR department's big budget that allowed this group to write the usual checks to 'influence' elected officials and government agencies to favor our industry. The most revealing parts of my involvement was the monitoring of what had been achieved with our PR dollars. It left me with a very jaded view of how some of our government works (not only ours, of course).

At several points I got embroiled in battling broadsides by overzealous interveners who were hell bent on fighting industry on all kinds of grounds, often ill-advised. One example was the now pretty much forgotten campaign against a key ingredient for a group of plastics known as PVC (polyvinylchloride). It is made by polymerizing vinyl chloride monomer (VCM). This had been done for years all over the world. Always concerned about workers' health, most industrial countries routinely monitored them, with no particular health issues detected from exposure to VCM..

Then out of the blue came an ambitious researcher at Mount Sinai Hospital with the name of Selikoff. Mining data from the chemical industries health records he had stumbled across a report that during a ten year period, eight out of about 400,000 chemical workers had developed a lethal cancer called angiosarcoma of the liver. Whether they had been exposed to VCM or not was not made clear. Based on this statistic he set into motion a campaign to ban all VCM manufacture (which would have put an end to electrical insulation, airplanes and medical devices like intravenous tubing). All hell broke lose.

I was asked to participate in Congressional hearings on this matter. One of our panel members asked a simple question: "If eight out of 400,000 chemical workers, over ten years, had developed this cancer, what is the incidence of the same cancer in the rest of the population?" The answer by Selikoff: "I do not know, and I do not care". You would think that this blunt statement would have put an end to the discussion, but it did not. The PVC industry was forced to spend an enormous amount of money (and time) to change its PVC manufacturing systems under new rules meant to eliminate this bad cancer, but nothing changed. Ten years later the industry data showed the same cancer incidence among its workers - and as it turned out, this was actually not much different from the incidents of this cancer in the entire US population, now being monitored by the NIH.

Later on I saw much of this type of scenario repeated in our industry's struggle against unfounded attacks on plastics and later on nuclear power by environmentalists who most of the time had very little knowledge of the facts. But for many of these self-appointed 'guardians of the public' facts usually do not matter.

My work in these industry associations (all honorary positions) and my giving lectures at our leading engineering schools were an excellent preparation for my many Board memberships in my later years. For ten years I chaired Wangner Corporation, a German-Italian industrial company in the paper machinery business. Their Italian partner was based in Venice which gave us plenty of reason to get to know this unique place.

In 1982 I was elected Director of the Plastics Institute of America (PIA). This was an industry-sponsored organization to help American engineering schools in developing better opportunities for students interested in making plastics technology their life careers. It gave me a long-awaited opportunity to step back into academia. I became very active in establishing sensible plastic technology curriculums at a number of US engineering school, first at the venerated Hoboken based Stevens Institute of Technology, and then at the much larger Lowell campus of Massachussets University where my long-time friend Prof.Nick Schott had built an exemplary Plastics Technology Department to become known world-wide. With the help of others from the plastics industry we equipped these engineering schools with production-size plastics processing machinery so that students could get 'hands-on' experience to complement their instructions that often were one-sidedly theoretical. I was invited as guest lecturer at a number of other engineering schools. I thoroughly enjoyed being a teacher once again, albeit part-time only.

At one point I was elected as the plastics industry's 'ambassador' to Eastern European engineering schools to promote academic exchanges, at a time when the 'Iron Curtain' and the Cold War were still very much a reality. I will never forget the cordial reception by the faculty at the University of Zagreb! For them it was like a whiff of fresh air in their drab Stalinistic existence. Some exquisite sets of precious cut crystal from those trips still adorn our home.

These interactions with people who had just a few years ago emerged from life under communism were eye-opening. It showed that in a mere two generations of brain-washing the mind-set of the "Easterners" was almost irreversibly molded into something very strange and also menacing to us Westerners. Some of their total lack of understanding of how to act as free people sometimes could almost be humerous, in a macabre way. Example: under the communists East Berlin was a very drab and miserable place but in true fashion the communists tried to build one huge show-piece, a big hotel complex on the formely world-famous Alexanderplatz. Needless to say, while huge and imposing in its Stalinistic style, after the re-unication of Germany it needed updating. West German capital and new management took over, and after two years of major re-vamping the Hotel am Alexanderplatz once again was the first class luxury hotel that the world had known in the old days.

Everything seemed to run well with the hotel until one day a few worker representatives requested a meeting with the newly appointed West German general manager. Sure, he said, what's on your mind? Well, these workers said, we understand that now that we are re-united with the rest of Germany, their laws about the requirements of our work place must apply, and one of these laws provides that each and every work-place must have a direct line of sight to the outside (true), but our group is in the basemment and we do not see the outside from there. Upon which the manager confirmed, yes, of course, you are entitled to better offices with outside windows. Ok, but tell me, who are you, anyway? Well, they said *"we are the telephone surveillance group. We listen in to all of our guests' telephone conversations"*. So, for more than two years after the end of the communist regime these workers faithfully continued what they had been trained for, with perfect performance of what they still felt was their legitimate duty to their fatherland, totally untouched by the fact that everything had changed. Had they not come up with their request for a better workplace they might still be there today, doing their 'duty', who knows! (A true story.)

The South German Industrial Safety Board elected me to Chair their US company, TUV America, reporting to our long time family friend Karl Eugen Becker, with great times working with this group in his beloved Munich. Then I became the US "Corresponding Member" of VDI, the all-encompassing German engineering society, with life tenure. And when the German WP group was broken up I took over the chair of the spin-off US Draiswerke company where I worked together with the former VP at WPC, Dieter Gras. Eventually we got the Michael Werner heirs to sell this company to its President, Gisbert Schall. When Gisbert got ready to retire I helped him sell this company to the Swiss Buehler Group.

All the untold hours I had dedicated to my association work and to teaching at Stevens Institute, Rutgers and Rensselear and others had paid of. Above all, it gave me tremendous satisfaction to be able to make my contribution - and my mark in my academic specialty of technology management. I met so many remarkable people with Francesca standing right next to me. She often played the role of the charming hostess, even helping sometimes to overcome tensions over controversial issues. She enjoyed, above all, the Bahama Board meetings with Gisbert Schall and his wife Iris, where our good friend Michael  Werner would hold court in his penthouse condo with his eccentric and legendary (third) wife Karina.

All this made for a very full life, together, in this quite rarified atmosphere of industrial and academic leadership.

My work went well. We lived the good life - managing growing and successful businesses, travelling all over the Western world and sometimes Asia, with Francesca on my side, holding everything together. We had made a dream come true - we had four healthy sons all at college now, great homes, with lots of friends and relatives coming and going.

But family life had to take first place.

Phases of our Lives

A Family of our own

"Be there for each other, no matter what life brings to you".

Phases of our Lives

Home, sweet Home

As I was pursuing my career, Francesca gave me her unwavering support. She kept the family going and, so to speak, covered my back, relieving me from having to worry about the home, about our sons and about our place in the community while I had to concentrate on doing my work.

Francesca was the one who always found the right home for us, furnished them with her unfailing impeccable taste (as her St.Barths friend Kattia DuBourg would say: "pas de clash!") and selected - and created - wonderful art.

Her first challenge came when we returned from Mexico and Germany. Highly pregnant with Eric we had to find a new home in a hurry - having sold our lovely Westport home which was just a bit too far for a daily commute to my New Jersey office.

Francesca found just the right place, a large ranch style house in Wyckoff, ready to move in just in time for baby Eric's arrival. High above the street, with a big wooded yard and a huge downstairs play room, it was complete with a room for nanny Maria whom we brought with us from Mexico, as soon as we had gotten her papers. Just a little over a year after Eric, we greeted David Roland into our world, and Francesca now had four little boys to mother, with 'three

under three' for a while.

Our nine years there were almost ideal for our toddler and grade school sons, with a very safe home and backyard, or so we thought. Until one year old Christoph found a way down our long driveway

and into the middle of the street making it on his butt all the way down two full blocks where the neighbors called us to retrieve him. Or two year old Eric falling down the back stairs and breaking his

collar bone, and only a few weeks later losing two of his teeth in the pavement falling over his bike's handle bars. Our pediatrician was called to check on our parenting ......

In this home we started the long parade of family get-togethers and neighborhood parties. Now almost fifty years later some of our friends still remember Francesca's annual Easter egg hunt. Everyone was anxiously hoping for an invitation!

After a wait of nine years we finally found our dream house on Franklin Lake where we would live for the next 25 years. Francesca master-minded a sweeping re-model, adding a huge downstairs space for play and entertainment and designing a stunning swimming pool.

It was the type of home I always wanted - something like a year around resort, with glorious summers, lots of out-door living space and swimming, and in New Jersey's cold winters, even ice skating parties on the frozen lake.

There were the most elegant dinners with Francesca's famous dinner settings that could rival the best of the Plaza.

And informal feast in our courtyard, next to the lake, shaded by our huge ash trees.

Often Francesca would be on the grill to feed a dozen or so ravenous teenagers, or for the annual Strauss Ball.

There never was any shortage of great family celebrations and even dinners on the lake, in our row boats!

We also wanted a second home - for fun, for investment and for a family refuge in case of emergency. Having lived through wars and economic calamities I believed it was important to always have some place of our own to fall back on. First, I wanted a farm nearby, but we never could find the right one. We decided instead on a beach house in Loveladies (!), one of the very the best parts of the New Jersey shore.

In all these New Jersey homes we hosted summer-long visitors from Germany, relatives and sons and daughters of my business contacts reciprocated by our sons visiting them in turn. In good European fashion, they would stay often for months on end. Francesca was the ever patient and gracious hostess for all of them. There were the Becker sisters Sylvia and Nicola, for Francesca like the daughters we never had. Then came Andy and Steffi Kuehltau (Andy would get love-sick over our friends' the LaRovere's daughter), then my Rohrbach nieces Michaela,

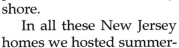

Ilona and Alexandra, and the family of my buddy from Gymnasium, Karl Schuelj, and many more, plus the friends they brought with them. Our lake-side home offered an ideal place for these teenagers, and Francesca became like a mother to them.

After Anneliese's divorce from her architect husband

Johannes, her sons, Cajatan and Claude spent many months in or Franklin Lakes home. Both had been very upset by their family's upheavals. In order to help them regain their self-confidence we arranged jobs for them with our PR firm and payed for their upkeep. It helped them to start excellent careers back in Switzerland.

With most of them we lost contact over the years, but some turned into life-long friends. The Beckers reciprocated by hosting son Wolf in Munich, treating him like the son they did not have. My long-time friend (and President of WP Germany) became Wolf's mentor. He arranged for Wolf to get his first job after graduation with the world-class Linde engineering company, headquartered in a Munich suburb with the unlikely name of Hoellsriegelskreut. In roaming through the Europe of the late 80ies, Christoph took full advantage of our connections. Eric and David thoroughly enjoyed themselves as frequent guest in the Ockers' grand home. The Rohrbach crowd would give us a warm reception whenever we ventured there with our family.

Finally, once my business involvements made my work schedule less demanding we took the big plunge and bought a villa in the Caribbean, on the French island of St. Bartholomew (in the US generally known as St. Barths). There were many, many visits to all kinds of other Caribbean islands and resorts before we decided on St. Barths. It all had started in the early 70s with Board meetings and with our WPC annual company meetings, all at top resorts. Francesca always volunteered to first scout these places, organized everything from accommodations, meeting venues, meals and entertainment. We got to know the islands very well.

We saw that every one of these islands was in fact very different from each other. It all depended who had 'colonized' them. The British 'bequeathed' them their bureaucracy and their two-class social structure, creating very fancy resorts that were 'Golden Ghettos' like the swank Caneel Club, but surrounded by abject poverty. As colonizers the Dutch and the Danes were more laissez-faire, and the French, of course, always more egalitarian. Then it depended whether there were plantations, which meant populating the islands with slaves brought over from Africa.

When we first started to explore the Caribbean, travel was often quite primitive. But it was great fun going 'island hopping' on quaint - and sometimes quite rickety - passenger ferries (like the "Bomba-Charger"!)or on float planes. In the modern age of jet airplanes and helicopters, all this is different now.

The small island of St. Barths had no plantations, therefore all the 'natives' were original French from Normandy, having arrived on this island in the late 1700s. For us it was just like living in a small town in the South of France. It was also not 'developed' like so many other Caribbean islands, much to their detriment. In St.Barths you find no high rise condos, no casinos, not even a golf course, but above all, no poverty and no crime. It was just pleasant Caribbean living in a casual elegant French ambiance. Being French speaking, I felt very much at home.

We bought a somewhat simple villa, for its location with its indescribably stunning view. Francesca got to work and made it into one of the greatest villas on this fashionable island, only to see it almost entirely destroyed by Hurricane Luis. Francesca was there with our sons Christoph, Eric and David during this ordeal. I had left just a day before its outbreak on BioTech business in Mexico. For a week there was no more contact with the island - I was frantic. I made it back via St.Thomas, on a very small two-seater plane that transported an outsized electric emergency generator that weight down this little plane, barely making it up into the still turbulent air. The storm had lasted three full days and did enormous damage. When I landed, everything was either black from burnt trees or white from salt water whipped up by the storm. Not accepting defeat, Francesca re-built it to be even more glamourous.

It became our winter home, the place where son Wolf would get married. Also it was the place where son David discovered the

Harvard-sponsored medical school on the nearby island of Saba, and this started him on his long and arduous road to becoming an MD. Truly, St.Barth became so important in the lives of all of us. It was with many tears that we had to leave this island paradise when

Francesca got seriously ill from heat and sun exposure. The main culprit was too much niacin to control cholesterol. But St. Barths did add so much to all of our family and our friends.

Most think of St.Barths the place for the 'rich and famous', and to a large extent this is true. However, this did not really constitue the essence of the ilsand. In the time we lived there it was still the place of casual French elegance where you could drive around in an open car, never even thinking of locking it, where there were no venders bothering you on the beaches and no shanties - none. Most of the elegant hill-side villas were owned by 'continental' French upper middle-class families and, of course, by prosperous old -time French settlers whose families had lived there for two hundred years, having settled on the island in the aftermath of the French revolution - after many generations of having eeked out a modest living from fishing and small farms they still control the island politically and they own most of the now thriving downtown real estate. They are the ones who still safeguard the particular St. Barths ambiance and the local culture and successfully enforce law and order, supported by a few metropolitan French gendarmes who tolerate no nonsense from any one. For the rare perpetrator there is swift justice - just leave the island, NOW. It works.

Of course there were the celebrities but the unwritten rule was that you would not take notice, to leave them alone to enjoy their vacations. Seeing Dave Letterman jogging, dining out at Maya's with Tom Hanks sitting at the table next to you, or Sean Connery making eyes at Francesca from a few tables away at La Marine were to be taken as 'normal' events not to be reacted to. The traditional French egalitarianism would come through to every one's comfort.

However, for us there was some quite unintended 'rubbing of shoulders' with visiting celebrities. One sunny day we went on a day sail on the 'Ne me Quitte Pas' catamaran with our friends John and Barbara Witt to go snorkeling at a nearby island. As we were about to take off a couple stepped up and asked whether they could join us and as it was expected we said yes. We spent a delightful day together with good food, many planters punches, good laughs and conversation - seemingly people just like us. At the end of the day they asked for all kinds of recommendation about beaches, about where to dine and all that, upon which Francesca invited them to visit us at our villa. The Witts took us aside and excitedly told us who this couple was: Barry Levinson of TV and movie screen writing and directing fame. For me it 'went in one ear and out the other' as I never paid much attention to the Holiwood crowd. The Levinsons did show up for a few drinks and of course I took part in the conversation and with my legendary lack of tact told Barry, the accomplished screen writer, that "I do not understand why here in America we can't find enough good writers and therefore have to go abroad......." Wow. Nevertheless they left as newly found friends!

Another day we were at Gouverneur's Beach snorkling to look in on 'our'octopus when Francesca unexpectedly got stung by some jellyfish. Leaving the water I went to the car to get some soothing lotion for her. While I was away for a few minutes a couple came running to Francesca, totally nude (that particular beach was 'topless' but not nude) gesticulating wildly and in broken English made Francesca understand that the woman had been stung by a jellyfish, just like her. Francesca tried to calm them down, looking for the French word for jellyfish. In her still imperfect French all she could think of was to say "c'etait un poisson de.....*marmelade*, de...*confiture*" which added immensely to the confusion - until I returned to tell them the French name (meduse). We proceeded then with the usual chit-chat about the best places for this and that, and parted. Only then it occurred to us: they were Roberto Benigni and his diminuitive wife Nicoletta who had just a few days earlier received an 'Oskar' for their performance in the movie "It is a Beautiful Life"(when he was so excited that he clambered over a few rows of seats to get onto the stage for his Oskar).

By the way, the 'written rule' for journalists was not even to write about visiting celebrities until they had already left the island. It helped greatly to ensure every one's privacy, not just for the celebrities.

In a strange way we got confronted there with a perplexing example of US 'States Rights' politics. Living for most of the year in St.Barths as official residents of France (St. Barths is a part of France in every respect) we thought it appropriate to obtain French driver licenses. We walked into the Sub-Prefect's quaint colonial style office overlooking the picturesque Gustavia harbor and, with great self-confidence asked him to issue us French driver licenses on the strenght of our New Jersey ones. Somewhat apologetically he told us that he could not do this "because France does not have a reciprocity agreement *with the State of New Jersey*". By way of explanation he confirmed that such reciprocity agreements did exist with most States of the Union but not with New Jersey. It was the first time we became aware of this strange state of affairs - each of our States still has the prerogative of doing its own thing on the international scene. Are we not "The *United* States of America"?

Not withstanding this interesting twist we became very much a part of the island's social life. A close friendship developed with our neighbors, above all the O'Keefes 'next door'. Peter had come to the island in the '60ies with an enterprising and artistic group, among others Jimmy Buffet of "Margaritaville" fame. At that time St.Barths was the quintessential new place for young people who wanted a simple life on an island that was not yet 'discovered'. He had singlehandedly built a truely Caribbean estate that was the envy of many of us newcomers. His wife Laurence became Francesca's best friend there. When their daughter Clara was born we we there to receive them at the airport when they brought their newborn back from the bigger French island Martinique (no birth were allowed then on St. Barth because there was no hospital there). At Clara's baptism in St.Barth's spendid colonial-time church we were asked to become Clara's god-parents. We are still in close touch with this most interesting family with Clara now studying in one of France's most prestigious university, and son Julian making a name for himself as St.Barths' most sought-after entertainer!

Wherever we were, we welcomed many, many friends and relatives to partake in our good fortunes. Of course, all this visiting made a huge amount of work for Francesca, but it had its big rewards. Now in our old age we are looking back at all our previous homes where so much living took place. Sharing our homes with so many guests showed our love that came with them. They are the things wonderful memories are made of.

<O>

Francesca's many Talents

Our own family life became very full with our sons' schools and athletics, with skiing trips to Grey Rocks, trips to explore America's great places. We became active in our sons' schools and in our Church's youth groups. We were a part of the community - just as we said we would.

Francesca showed her many talents. She could be the most charming party host, the most thoughtful mother, and the triumphant 'Belle of the Ball'.

Or the one frolicking in grand style on the snowy lake! Soon Francesca would become famous for her great dinner parties, for friends, relatives and, increasingly, for my business contacts. Much better to invite them to our home than to spend endless evenings in restaurants. Our four sons always were included in these events, much for their benefit, getting exposed to people from many different backgrounds.

Entertaining family and guests was second nature to her - she could do it in many different ways - often very elegant, with table settings more elegant than 'Town and Country', and often simple and rustic, but always with great 'flair'. And always, always, delicious. After nanny Maria had left us to get married, her friend from Mexico, Isabel, stayed with us for over twenty years, helping with the chores of running a big house, innumerable guests and riding herd over our teenage boys when we were away. Francesca became a superb manager of a very substantial household.

EVENTS

Ramapo College arts displayed

Sculpture students at Ramapo College will display their work in an unusual exhibit in the new state college's library from May 2-17 during regular library hours.

The Ramapo students' work will be joined by area senior citizens who have participated in the college-sponsored "Art on the Outside" project which is funded by a Department of Higher Education grant under Title I of the Community Service Act. The exhibit will include sculptures in cement, plaster, wire, wood and clay. Admission is free and the public is invited to attend.

From May 13-May 20, Ramapo College will sponsor an unusual art exhibit in the lobby of the college auditorium featuring the work of imprisoned, mentally disturbed and the elderly.

The exhibit will represent the work of six area institutions including the Rockland Psychiatric Center in Orangeburg, N.Y.; The Central Bergen and West Bergen Mental Health Centers; Bergen County Jail Annex in Hackensack; The Ridgewood Nursing Home and Catholic Family Services.

The program is part of Ramapo College's successful "Art on the Outside" Program which is funded by a grant from the Department of Higher Education of New Jersey under Title I of the Community Service Act.

Professor Judith Peck's Ramapo students, in groups of three or four, travel to each of the six local institutions to assist in the art workshops which are designed for improvement of self-image and a sense of personal accomplishment among the people who are in situations of physical and emotional confinement.

The exhibit is free and the public is invited to attend.

Francesca Mack, a Ramapo College art student from Wyckoff puts the finishing touches on a wire and plaster sculpture which will be shown in an all-student sculpture exhibit from May 2 - May 17 in the Ramapo College Library. The artists, including area senior citizens, will show a variety of media including sand castings, wood carvings and found object sculptures. The public is invited.

That did not prevent her from continuing her art studies. At Ramapo College she found an outstanding artist teacher, Prof. Judith Peck, who ran a very well known painting and sculpture studio.

Francesca would become her star student, creating an number of first class paintings and very expressive sculptures. Juggling

being a mother to four very active boys, deeply involved in her husbands's business, and running a home with an endless parade of guests she would work long hours to put her vivid imagination into amazing pieces of art. Whenever Prof. Peck would stage an exhibit of her and her students' work, Francesca's inevitably took center stage.

Putting her growing knowledge of the world of art into practice Francesca also became drawn into a most fascinating episode involving a world-class painting by Gustav Klimt, "The Fulfillment", a part of his trilogy "The Kiss" and "The Expectation". This story started when our good friend and neighbor, Freddy Grunwald, had found out that this painting was displayed prominently in Strasbourg's famous Art Museum. It had been confiscated by the Nazis from his father's Vienna art gallery. Freddy, of course, wanted it back.

Freddy remembered well that it had hung in his parents' Vienna living room. Like many other dispossessed former owners of significant art, he wanted it back - not for its enormous value (his family did not need the money) - for him, it was a matter of principle. But his efforts ran into a lot of complications that unfortunately were typical for many such restitution attempts. First, he needed someone who could handle the correspondence and the negotiations - all in French, of course. Freddy knew that I spoke French and asked me to help.

Francesca and I went to Strasbourg (half an hour from Gengenbach!) only to find out that the Strasbourg Art Museum was not about to part with its prized possession. The citizens of Strasbourg were proud to have it in their city and put pressure on the Mayor and the City Council to resist Freddy's request.

In an ill disguised attempt to derail Freddy's efforts, the local Strasbourg judge demanded tangible 'proof of ownership'. Everybody knew that this would be impossible to get - to cover their tracks, the Nazis had routinely destroyed all ownership records. Fortunately there were markings on the painting's frame and on its shipping crate that could be traced back to Freddy's father's gallery. Afraid of the local politics, the judge declared them to be 'insufficient circumstantial evidence.'

We went on to the French Court of Appeals in Colmar which took a broader view and noted also that the price at which the Museum had acquired the Klimt in 1959 was "derisively" low - $7,000. Even at that time, it would have been worth at least thirty times more, which should have made the Museum doubt the legitimacy of the seller. This Court ordered the

painting to be turned over to Freddy. We threw a victory party for the Grunwalds who thanked us very much for all the work Francesca and I had put into the arduous recovery process.

Once again in possession of this great piece of art, he and his wife Ilse decided to donate it to a charitable organization supporting promising young artists. She had decided that for her this world honored painting was "too glitzy" to hang in their home, which was already filled with many other originals by Klimt, Schiele and Kokoschka, smaller paintings that Freddy's father had been able to smuggle out of Vienna as the Nazis were taking over the country.

For many years we were very active followers of the New York Metropolitan Opera and of the New York Philharmonic, holding four coveted tenth row center seats for many years. In 1993, shortly after being named the Philharmonic's music director, Kurt Masur took a small group of his supporters with him on his orchestra's tour to Eastern Europe, just after these 'Iron Curtain' countries had opened once more to us 'Westerners'. He took us to Poland, from Krakow to Warsaw and the former Breslau, and then on to Prague. Playing his orchestra's hallmark Fouth Bruckner Symphony in every one of their grand music halls was received with enthusiasm by the 'Easteners' who had been shut off from the world for so long.

While in Poland Francesca tried hard to connect to her distant relatives from both the Greskiewicz and the Klocko side, with very limited success. The few actual addresses we had from previous visits by her Pennsyvania aunts were not very welcoming to us. Apparently they feared that we were visiting Poland to do what so many Westerner were trying at that time: to re-possess properties that had been expropriated during the Communist regime. No amount of explaining helped. They just did not want to meet with us. Maybe we also were not able to really communicate with them, our Polish language abilities were nearly non-existent at that point.

Through the Philharmonic we met some most interesting Polish notables. One of them was Kristof Paderewski, a decendent of very prominent Polish aristocrats, noted contemporary composer and music director of Krakow's Symphony. Francesca and his elegant wife became instant friends. She showed us their magnificent country estate and told us of the very hard times during the war and how she and her mother had single-handedly done the actual rebuilding of their ruined home. On this memorable trip we were given access to so many cultural sites that without being a part of the celebrated Philharmonic would not be accessible to us at all. We learned so much about Poland's amazing history and its cultural

life. We will never forget the glamourous reception in our honor at Krakow's ancient Jagellonian University, the very oldest in Europe!

And then, quite unexpectedly, we were also drawn into the world of professional tennis. In 1978 Ramapo College had started an annual women's tennis tournament to take place during the weeks before the big 'US Open' in New York's Flushing Meadows. Ramapo would attract the world's top women tennis players who conveniently used this tournament as a warm-up for the forthcoming US Open. As if our lives were not full enough Francesca readily followed the call to open homes like ours for these tennis stars, who preferred staying with families rather than in hotels. Year after year we would host some of the most prominent

tennis stars - we fondly remember 'Peanut' Lui, Annemarie Fernandez and Gabriela Sabatini, and saw Steffi Graf and Martina Navrotilova taking a dip in our pool before sitting down on our deck to one of Francesca's savory meals.

We discovered that their stardom had not necessarily 'spoiled' them. They were just delightful young women, grateful for the respite from their grueling competition in the warmth of a family. Some became life-long friends - more than thirty years later we still are in touch with Peanut, now living around the corner from son Wolf, in San Francisco. Wolf became very close to Tracy Austin. He would date her for two years, on and off, during his time at Carnegie Mellon, while getting his MBA.

Our tennis player friends would give us 'Coaches Passes' with access to everything at the US Open, including the 'back-stage' scene. It opened up an entirely new world for us. It also gave us a new respect for their struggles. Watching them play was a fascinating and often nerve-wrecking experience. It was very personal. We were enthralled with their wins, and we suffered with them in their defeats. And every so often they would invite me to hit the ball with them at our club. They would make me look very good by carefully placing the ball so that I could return it well. Watching this spectacle my tennis friends were in awe how much my game had improved......

These were great days for all of us. Francesca has this amazing gifts for making just about everything into some form of pleasant and interesting experience. No wonder that people would flock to her to be included in our lives.

Phases of our Lives

The Crowning

When the time came for our sons to marry, Francesca's talent to make everything around her beautiful once more came to the fore. With her loving devotion she would make each of their wedding days (and their honeymoons) such joyous events to make their start into married life a memorable one.

First was son Wolfgang, marrying Kathy Hanson on St. Bart's Saline Beach (much to the consternation of her very conservative family). There was also an incredible stroke of luck in our timing - just a few days later, after all the wedding guest had left, the terrible hurricane Luis hit the island with devastating force.

Then came David's and Amanda's wedding on Vashon Island, with such a fun celebration with the Butcher family and friends. Little Sophie was such a cute flower girl! They would move to North Dakota for David's residency and then, after some hesitation, to Anchorage in Alaska, opening entirely new horizons for all of us. Their little Audrey and Adam keep visiting us, and we are always so happy to reciprocate.

Eric and Eden romantically eloped to get married in a civil ceremony in England's historic city of Bath. Their commitment was confirmed with a large gathering of her and our family, and friends, at the great Alderbrook resort on gorgeous Hood Canal. They settled in Seattle where Eric is pursuing his career in a leading position at Amazon. The frequent visits by little Adeline and her twin brothers, Adrian and Anderson warm our hearts.

Then Opa was asked to officiate at the marriage of Christoph and Lisa Friede in the elegant Olympic Four Seasons Hotel, followed by a reception in Seattle's gloriously remodeled King Station. They, too, live in Seattle, and we are so happy to see them often, with their twins, Lily and Lucas, who like to take us on their legendary 'expotitions'.

Finally, when son Wolf re-married and tied the knot with Nicole Alvino, our good friends, the Witts, opened up their great Napa Valley estate as the venue for the wedding celebration. Francesca gave a most romantic and poetic outdoor feast in the middle of the vineyards. Their sons Little Wolf, Roland and Conrad always greet us so with such enthusiasm when we visit them in San Francisco.

For all these wonderful events Francesca organized the most elegant and imaginative settings. We were happy that we could do this. Not that we were ever flush with money - we had to work very hard to create our modest level of prosperity. It was just that sharing whatever we had was very much in Francesca's and my make-up. And we hope that our sons' families will be of the same mind when their turn will come. In the meantime we are in 'grandparent

heaven' as we are watching our eleven wonderful grandchildren growing up and loving us as we love them. We could not wish for a more pleasant old age in our chosen retirement home in Seattle.

We keep very close relations with Francesca's siblings and their families. Once more we took all of our sons and their families to my

home town Gengenbach to let them "sense their roots" with photos taken on a sweltering summer day in front of the Rathause where for me it all had begun.

For us there is no better place and time to reminisce about the 'Phases of our Lives'. It means a lot to us. We hope that reading about them it will also mean something to our readers when they will take time out to contemplate the many efforts that go into a life time of relationships:

Above everything else - be there for each other, always.

That makes it all worth it.

"There is room in the smallest cottage
for a happy loving pair."
—Friedrich Schiller

Epilogue

Looking back you can ask a lot of questions about our long lives. We often do.

It's easy to ask. It's not that easy to find the answers. It's not easy to see the whole picture when so much has happened.

Did we really make the best use of all the opportunities that life offered to us?

Were we always as charitable to our beloved ones, to our friends, to those in need?

Did we always do enough to protect ourselves, and those around us, from injustice, from unnecessary hardships and from unwarranted disappointments?

Life is so full of events and issues that it is a hopeless undertaking to pass something like 'summary judgement'.

I have heard people say:"Look, he came here with nothing, and now see what he has achieved". Well, it is true I did not come with a sack full of money, but I did not come empty handed at all - I already had a first class education, and I was brought up in a home that instilled excellent values. And I had Francesca as my loving spouse who was a true life companion, not only sharing everything with me, but working alongside with me in all my endeavors, and building the best family I could possibly have hoped for.

I thought it very worth while to write about these phases of our lives. It hopefully will help us, and our readers, to pass judgement on what we did, what we did well, and perhaps what we could have done better.

I also hope that our readers will find my writings interesting as a document of the times in which we lived and worked. Ours was a life full of surprises and sometimes great danger, and thankfully, also so joyful and uplifting. For that, we are grateful beyond measure.

<O>

Phases of our Lives

Proof

Made in the USA
Charleston, SC
24 October 2016